£7.50

The Theatre Student

PUPPETRY

THE ULTIMATE DISGUISE

The Theatre Student

PUPPETRY
THE ULTIMATE
DISGUISE

George Latshaw

PUBLISHED BY
RICHARDS ROSEN PRESS, INC.
NEW YORK, N.Y. 10010

Published in 1978 by Richards Rosen Press, Inc.
29 East 21st Street, New York, N.Y. 10010

First Edition

Library of Congress Cataloging in Publication Data

Latshaw, George.
  Puppetry.

   (The Theatre student)
   Bibliography: p.
   SUMMARY: Discusses aspects of puppet theatre such
as design, voices and sound effects, characterization, stages,
and playwriting.
   1. Puppets and puppet-plays. [1. Puppets and
puppet-plays] I. Title.
PN1972.L35   791.5'3   77–23801
ISBN 0–8239–0363–X

Manufactured in the United States of America

ABOUT THE AUTHOR

GEORGE LATSHAW is a master puppeteer known throughout the United States and the world. His work for motion pictures and television includes the musical-drama version of James Thurber's *The Great Quillow* for NBC; *The Convertible Crocodile,* a part of a CBS-TV special; and assistance to Walton and O'Rourke with the hand puppets in MGM's *Lili.*

He has twice represented the United States at the International Puppet Festival in Great Britain. His commissions include three from the Theatre Arts Department of the Detroit Institute of Arts to design and direct experimental productions with the Detroit Symphony. He wrote and directed *To Dream a Dinosaur* and adapted Pinocchio for live actors and marionettes. His written works include *AJLA Children's Theatre Manual,* a chapter on Puppetry in *Children's Theatre and Creative Dramatics,* and numerous articles in periodicals.

Mr. Latshaw served as consultant on Children's Theatre for the Association of Junior Leagues from 1960 to 1972, and as special consultant to the Department of Education in Puerto Rico. He is a former president of the Puppeteers of America and a former board member of the Children's Theatre Conference and UNIMA (International Puppetry Association)–USA Center. He has been a member of the Board of Advisors for the United States Center of the International Association of Theatres for Children and Youth. In 1971 he was the recipient of the Jennie Heiden Award for professional excellence in Children's Theatre from the American Theatre Association.

Mr. Latshaw lives with his wife and two sons (the latter aid him in many of his productions) at their home in Macedonia, Ohio.

PREFACE

When I was a child, my idea of heaven was to be taken out to a "show." The first one I saw was such a revelation that I drew a picture of it on my blackboard to fix it in my mind forever. That sketch showed the proscenium, the footlights, the actors onstage (one of them balancing a stack of books on his head), and the furniture, but no drawing could reveal the secret meaning of that experience. I had thought "pretending" was a private part of childhood. Suddenly I had seen it happen in a public place in front of grown-ups, and no one had thrown a fit or tried to stop it. It was too good to be true. The "grown-ups" on stage pretended, the grown-ups in the audience "pretended" right back, and we all had fun. A "show" performed a miracle, for it set aside a time and place where actors and audience, young and old, could make believe together. After that, I could not imagine anything more exciting (in this world or the next) than to be in the audience for a play, a concert, a circus, a vaudeville, or a puppet show. Each variation on performance was joy compounded.

In those days, movies were in black and white, radio was on the rise, and television was unknown. It was the heyday of the traveling show, and the stage was a Mt. Olympus on which the reigning gods appeared "live" and "in person" to thrill us with dazzling displays of talent. Performers always came across larger than life. So marvelous, so magnetic were they that I wanted to leap out of my seat to join them on the stage, feeling that if I went "up there" they would not stop, and that the show would last forever.

More than once I was dragged up the aisle, protesting, when it was time to leave. I would promise anything to get inside a theatre, knowing I would forget my promise as soon as I sat down in the dark. Who could bear to depart if there was to be a second show? The costumes might be different, the acts might change, the lights might work another way. Even if it all turned out to be the same, any excuse would do to prolong the pleasure of sitting through it one more time. I don't remember ever leaving a theatre willingly when I was young.

My growing-up years were filled with varied entertainments, from the Clare Tree Major children's theatre productions to the Tuesday Musical Series, The Vienna Boys Choir, the Joos Ballet, and the Folies Parisienne. Interspersed with these events were memorable puppet performances by Helen Haiman Joseph, Sue Hastings, Rufus and Margo Rose, the Kingsland Marionettes, Walton & O'Rourke, C. Ray Smith's Olvera Street Marionettes, and the Lessellis. After seeing Alfred Lunt and Lynn Fontanne romp through *The Taming of the Shrew,* I knew that theatre had to be my life.

When I could not see a play or a puppet show, I would seek out books on those subjects in the Children's Room of the Akron Public Library. There a kind librarian introduced me to a stirring novel about the medieval guild system, which set my course toward being an apprentice in the arts. The Akron Jaycees furthered that interest, through the Junior Achievement program, by arranging career interviews with traveling professionals. I can say that I spoke to Ed Sullivan and Arthur Treacher before they were televised and franchised.

As a college freshman I wanted to major in everything all at once. That was not possible, and, even worse, I found that college theatre was not even on speaking terms with puppetry. These performance "twins" of my youth seemed like two high-spirited steeds, snorting and stomping, pulling in opposite directions, bucking and rearing, intent on galloping off on their separate ways. Since I refused to let go of either one, I held the reins and have been hanging on for dear life ever since.

It is my intent, in this book, to lead puppetry and theatre into the same ring at the same time; to parade them around together under the lights, noting what is similar while respecting what is unique. The focus will be on the performers, the actors and the puppeteers who are the life of their respective stages. In that sense, both are equal, for they are both human, and being human allows for infinite diversity. It is up to the performers to choose the degree to which they wish to be disguised.

If persons are a sum of their experience (and their attitudes toward that experience), then it is only fair to acknowledge the people and events that have shaped my thinking toward the writing of this book. To my mother, I owe more than I can say. She introduced me to the performing arts and puppetry. She made it possible for me to see whatever there was to see. I am also indebted to those artists who took to the road to play the towns where I lived. They inspired me to follow in their footsteps as soon as my age and skills would allow.

A career is always bolstered by the encouragement of special friends, and I would name Dr. Walter F. Tunks, Mabel Todd, Yetta Graham Mitchell, Dina Rees Evans, Winifred Ward, Clarence Murphy, Paul Eden, and Dr. Kenneth L. Jones. My wife, Pat, and my sons Christopher and Michael have been not only boosters but co-workers on recent projects.

I have learned much from those professionals with whom I have worked full-time or fleetingly: Mabel and Cedric Head, Helen Joseph, Martin Stevens, Alfred Wallace, Olga Stevens, Burr Tillstrom, Walton & O'Rourke, Wolo, John Conway, Jim Henson, Bob Huber, and Chalmers Dale. Others inspired through their innovative work: Marjorie Batchelder McPharlin, Basil Milovsoroff, Yves Joly, Georges Lafaye, Adam Kilian, Jan Wilkowski, and Sergei Obraztsov. The succession of Curators of Theatre Arts at The Detroit Institute of Arts, Adolph S. Cavallo, Gil Oden, and Audley M. Grossman, Jr., deserve special thanks for providing commissions to design and direct experimental works on a large scale. Dr. Nat Eek extended similar invitations to work on three productions at The University of Oklahoma, ranging from *Agamemnon* to the premiere of my play for live actors and puppets *To Dream a Dinosaur*.

Along the way there were inspiring teachers, among them Frank Bevan, Ed Cole, Frank McMullan, and Walter Pritchard Eaton of the Yale Drama School. They could challenge and encourage at the same time. "Doc" Evans steered me toward children's theatre and puppetry combined during my years as instructor and director of the Junior School at Cain Park. Dr. Walter H. Walters, now Dean of the College of Arts and Architecture, The Pennsylvania State University, extended the first invitation to teach in a Theatre Department at the college level. The Training Division of The Episcopal Diocese of Ohio furthered my understanding of what it is to teach and what it is to learn during a Province Five Lab in Experiential Education. It was an eye-opener, although Viola Spolin had been using the technique in Theatre Games for years! To enable students to discover that point of view which they alone can bring to their puppets is the joy and the reward of being a part of the educational process. It is my hope that each person reading this book will find something different in it to strengthen and expand a uniquely personal approach to puppetry.

Many years ago Jay Marshall, puppeteer, magician, and performer extraordinaire, was kind enough to suggest that I write down some of my workshop approaches for publication, but I did not pick up my cue. When Paul Kozelka repeated the suggestion, he demonstrated the infinite patience of a kindly prompter until I finally got my lines down. To have the subject of Puppetry included in the Theatre Student Series is my notion of landing in the best of both worlds.

George Latshaw

CONTENTS

The Theatre Student

PUPPETRY

THE ULTIMATE DISGUISE

Chapter I

THE HODGEPODGE HISTORY OF THE PUPPET

"The Puppets are coming! The Puppets are coming!" might turn out to be the "cue and cry" of the century. So pervasive are the puppets of today, it seems unlikely that anyone could pass through life without running into them at least once. People are meeting puppets in the most unexpected places, because the puppet explosion is a phenomenon of our own time. Even Snoopy was inspired to do a one-beagle hand (or paw?) puppet version of *War and Peace* in Schulz's Sunday strip.

The forward march of the marionette began in the 1920's, after World War I. The pace quickened during the 1930's and 1940's, and the family name was shortened to "puppet" instead of "marionette." Puppets entertained the troops on USO tours during World War II. The Giant Leap for puppets came in the 1950's when network television blasted them into the electronic age. Puppets took to television as if it were the new Shangri La. Who cared if these hardy survivors of ancient times were really thousands of years old? They certainly did not look their age. On camera, they were fresh and bright and full of fun. Puppets reveled in a visibility such as they had never known before. Their audience could be counted in the millions. From among the ranks came puppet celebrities and superstars the equal of any human entertainers. Puppets were sitting on top of the world at last.

Even before their conquest of television, puppets had spilled into the fields of education, recreation, advertising, public relations, psychology, therapy, and international diplomacy, as well as sex, politics, and religion. The more puppets diversified, the more they were asked to do, for there seemed to be no limit to their enterprise. Looking ahead, there is the new laser-based process of 3-D motion-picture holography for the puppets to explore. Who can predict what new careers are yet to come?

How have these audacious woodenheads managed to survive the good times and the bad through centuries to find success in the space age? It does seem an unlikely time. Our era is one of tension and upheaval brought about by the rapid pace of change. Tremors have shaken the foundations of the railroads, the cities, and even family life, while the puppets have grown stronger every day. Obviously they have developed a cosmetic facility for keeping up with the times. Invent a new material, and puppets snatch it up. Plastics, foam rubber, stretch-knits, fake furs, and stereo are all a part of the puppet scene. What is their secret? Is there some bond to humans that runs deeper than the outward appearance of things? A flashback may turn up the clues we need.

Puppets have dashed in and out of theatre history with all the zeal of the Marx Brothers going through a revolving door. "In, Out, Off and Away" seems to have been their motto. Hurl that insult! Throw that jibe! Get that laugh and begone!—never bothering to leave a name, date, or forwarding address. At times the puppet has been very close to the theatre of the day; at other times it has been very far afield. Some theatre historians are so annoyed by the hide-and-seek history of the puppet that they ignore it entirely when they write. True, the puppet lacks a straight, line-drive record of accomplishment down through the ages that would compare with theatre, music, or dance;

but the puppet has always been there—on stage, in the streets, and sometimes only in the showman's heart.

The origins of the puppet would take us back to antiquity. Born into the myth-making societies, half brothers to the Mask, these creatures served as messengers to mouth the words of men and gods.

By the time writers took note of such things, the puppets had embarked on a second career, as comic figures, to divert the mortals they once had held in awe. So popular were the puppets that a showman named Potheinos was allowed to perform with his marionettes in the great theatre of Dionysus in the 5th century B.C. On stage the actor and the marionette would have looked much alike. The masked actor was a magnifying mirror for the puppet, as the puppet was a miniature reflection of the man. Puppets borrowed farce themes from the actors, and the actors in turn borrowed movements and gestures from the puppets. Such exchanges between the actor and the puppeteer recur at scattered moments throughout history. These are moments only, of meeting, passing like an eclipse, and moving on. These performers are destined to orbit around similar, but separate, stars.

Following the Roman period, the puppets fade away, only to turn up later in the company of jugglers, acrobats, and dancing bears to entertain the simple folk. The puppet never had a place of permanence where audiences would flock to see the show. No matter. Perhaps it was the restless urge to see the world that kept the puppets on the move, or better still, the urge to have the World see Puppets!

During the Middle Ages puppets assisted in bringing religious teachings alive within the Church, until their sense of humor got so out of hand that they were booted into the street. Puppets had been there before, so it did not upset them to return. They were among friends, and they survived. Shakespeare mentions puppets in his plays. During an austere period following the Elizabethan age, actors were banned from performing on the stage, but the puppets were allowed to continue on their merry way—free from attack from everyone but the actors.

Puppeteers recognized a kindred spirit in the masked actors of the commedia dell'arte. Character types were strong and bold, the style was loose and free, and the same roles were repeated in many plots. One commedia character was held over to star upon the puppet stage: Punchinello, or Punch for short, who developed into the unbeatable half of Punch and Judy. In May, 1962, a ceremony was held to celebrate the 300-year run of his durable deviltry. A commemorative plaque on the portico of St. Paul's Church, Covent Garden (the Actors' Church), reads, "Near this spot Punch's Puppet show was first performed in England and witnessed by Samuel Pepys, 1662." Long live Mr. Punch!

The rough-and-tumble life of the European puppets made them resilient enough to survive without theatres to house them or playwrights to write for them. They entertained emperors and kings without losing their earthy antics for the street crowd. There is no doubt of the puppets' appeal to an earlier age, but that does not explain their power in today's world.

I have my own "creation myth" of how the puppet came to be. Imagine a primitive tribe reacting to thunder, lightning, fire, and flood as if these were caused by sinister forces roaming the world. To appease the furies that could bring death and destruction, there was a need to communicate with them—to speak and be spoken to. A name and a shape would be given to each god. These images, idols, and fetishes brought the furies into the visible world. To speak to the spirits required a wise man or shaman of the tribe. The shaman was an "instrument" through which the thoughts of the gods could be translated into words the tribe could understand. If the spirit spoke in the shaman's voice, it was because he had been selected to speak for the spirit world. If the fetish wished to move, it was the shaman's duty to assist in unobtrusive ways. This was not trickery, but a necessary "magic" to cope with the overwhelming fear of the unseen and the unknown. The shaman created the first puppets as dwelling places for the gods, and he was both servant and master of these creations. Imagine the therapeutic value of the shaman role, to be on both sides of the struggle, playing the aggressor and the aggrieved.

Primitive puppets were a link between the human and the spirit worlds. When the gods fell out of favor, the puppets remained, for they were experienced tour guides who could lead the living to whatever imagined world they wished to travel. I believe this is the secret of the puppets' enduring service to humanity. Puppets help us to see the unseen and to know the unknown in ways that are comic or comforting, according to our needs. Peter D. Arnott's marionettes evoke the essence of great theatre periods of the past. Bil Baird's marionettes simulate the moon walk for us to cover what the television cameras cannot show. Jim Henson's lovable monsters invite the young to venture into the unknown world of letters and numbers. Puppets today are doing what they have always done, providing a simulation device for exploring whatever inner or outer worlds the human mind can create.

Puppetry in the United States grew out of the European tradition of entertainment, rather than the American Indians' use of puppets and masks for ritual. Until the 20th century the puppet show was an occasional novelty reaching a limited audience. Today it has pushed beyond live performance to publication, organization, shift of media, shift of message, mass marketing, and psychology. These are a few highlights of the action.

In the beginning there was Tony Sarg, an artist-illustrator of the 1920's and 1930's who produced marionette shows. He used one career to promote the other, and for years his name was a synonym for the marionette. The Sarg studios begat the new professionals, who were Rufus and Margo Rose, Bil Baird, and Sue Hastings. And there was ferment. Helen Haiman Joseph directed marionette productions at The Cleveland Playhouse. Forman Brown and Harry Burnett teamed up as The Yale Puppeteers to pioneer a style of witty, adult puppetry. William Ireland Duncan and

Edward Mabley (The Tatterman Marionettes) mounted a superspectacular touring production of *Peer Gynt*. On the West Coast Ralph Chessé won acclaim for staging classic plays from the human theatre. And there was more ferment. Martin and Olga Stevens' repertoire included *The Passion Play, The Nativity,* and *St. Joan.* There was so much ferment that The Federal Theatre Project took puppeteers under its protective wing during the Great Depression of the 1930's.

After vaudeville died, puppet "acts" traveled with the big band shows that toured the same circuits. Walton & O'Rourke, Bob Bromley, and Frank Paris moved into the international nightclub field. Sid Krofft learned to skate in order to be the first to present his marionettes on ice in a New York revue. The situation was reversed during the 1975–76 season, when skaters in Shipstads & Johnson's *Ice Follies* donned costumes and learned to move and act like Henson's Muppets on *Sesame Street.*

World's Fairs have thrown a spotlight on puppets. At the Century of Progress in Chicago, Tony Sarg's company was the star; at the Great Lakes Exposition, the Tattermans topped the bill; and for the second New York World's Fair Bil Baird's show for Chrysler was No. 1. The Seattle World's Fair catapulted Sid and Marty Krofft's "Les Poupées de Paree" to Los Angeles and on to Hemis-Fair in San Antonio. The theme amusement parks that dot the country are mini-world's fairs. Worlds of Fun in Kansas City, Six Flags in several locales, and King's Island in Cincinnati have all used puppets to entertain the crowds. Even the Greatest Show on Earth, Ringling Brothers, Barnum and Bailey Circus, featured the inventive puppets of a talented clown during the walk-around.

In spite of all the places the puppet had appeared in person, it was the publishers who helped the puppet to "go public." The first "how-to" book by Tony Sarg cracked the code of silence that had existed for centuries. Old puppet showmen handed down their secrets from generation to generation. Security was so essential that family troupes would mask the backstage area so that stagehands and other performers could not see the figures or the devices by which they were controlled.

There is a story told about how Tony Sarg discovered the secrets. While he was a young artist in London, he attended a puppet performance and took a seat in the front row. After the house lights went out, he got down on his back to peek up through the proscenium to study the hidden part. From that view he was able to get enough information to launch his own career. His book appeared after he had established his reputation in the United States. About the same time, Helen Haiman Joseph wrote *A Book of Marionettes,* the first history to be published in English. Thus puppet information passed from a few professionals to a host of eager amateurs. The early trickle of publication has turned into a torrent. Plays, Inc. of Boston today makes a specialty of books on puppetry and has brought out U.S. editions of valuable books from abroad (see Bibliography).

Gordon Craig introduced his ubermarionette to the theatre world by publishing *The Mask* and *The Marionette.* In the U.S., Paul McPharlin's *Yearbooks* (1930–47) served as a unifying influence with their annual reports and pictures of the national and international scene. McPharlin's masterwork, *The Puppet Theatre in America: 1524 to Now,* was published posthumously in 1949. Marjorie Batchelder McPharlin added a supplement, *Puppets in America since 1948,* when the work was reissued by Plays, Inc., in 1969. Batchelder's *Puppet Theatre Handbook,* written originally as a manual for the armed services, is still a definitive resource on all phases of construction and production. Cyril Beaumont's pictorial surveys of international puppetry brought the world view to the reader's lap. *The Art of the Puppet* by Bil Baird is the most lavishly produced and handsomely illustrated book on puppetry to come from this country to date.

The libraries' role in acquiring and circulating new books has stimulated community interest, and a few institutions have added puppet shows to their story hours for children. Tom

Tichenor's program for the Nashville Public Library is a notable example. In Tampa, Florida, Virginia Rivers and her staff produce and perform puppet shows based on books. After opening at the Main Library, the plays are toured to branches throughout the city and county system. The Missouri State Library system honored the folk art of puppetry through a conference on "Puppetry and the Oral Tradition" in February, 1976.

As books had built bridges to information, organizations built bridges between people. The *Union Internationale de la Marionette* (UNIMA) was formed in 1929 to unite puppeteers of the world in a common concern for their art. The Puppeteers of America was organized a few years later. Now numbering more than 2,000 members in the United States, Canada, Mexico, and Puerto Rico, the organization provides a bimonthly magazine, *The Puppetry Journal,* edited by Don Avery; consulting services for members; and an annual national festival on a college or university campus each summer. William Ireland Duncan created the liaison with educational theatre. Archie Elliott, a businessman who is a fan of puppetry, served as President and Festival Chairman more than once and continues to act as adviser to the program chairpersons in setting up the annual meetings.

The animated film cartoons posed the first real threat to the puppet domain of fantasy. Live puppets were outclassed in every way by cartoon characters who blinked their eyes, cried tears, shaped their mouths to suit the words, wiggled fingers, squashed themselves flat as pancakes only to rise up and fill out again. Cartoons could dance any step, sing any song, and even invite live actors to perform in their two-dimensional world. Puppets tried to adapt to the animation technique by being photographed one frame at a time while the action was advanced slightly between shots. It was a painstaking and time-consuming process pioneered by George Pal's Puppetoons, and continued by Sutherland and Moore for a short time. Lou Bunin and a crew of American technicians were invited to France to train puppet filmmakers on a version of *Alice in Wonderland*. Unfortunately the release collided with Disney's cartoon *Alice* and the two films played movie houses within months of each other. Michael Myerberg produced Thornton Wilder's *Skin of Our Teeth* with live actors, then turned his attention to a puppet film of *Hansel and Gretel* with a script by Padraic Colum. The feature-length stop-action puppet film seems to have faded out of the picture in the United States due to its high cost and tedious pace. However the international stars in this field were Lotte Reininger, for her exquisite shadow films, and Jiri Trnka, whose productions of *The Emperor's Nightingale* and *Midsummer Night's Dream* found worldwide release.

The first puppet superstar came out of the golden age of radio, when the nation tuned in to hear Edgar Bergen spar with Charlie McCarthy on Sunday nights. The precedent for the puppet-human team was set right there, not just as a ventriloquist act, but because Charlie McCarthy had the brass and wit to take on all comers from the celebrity guest list. His running battle with W. C. Fields was one of the legendary feuds of the era. Bergen's success paved the way for other teams—Paul Winchell and Jerry Mahoney, and Shari Lewis and Lamb Chop.

In the early days of television, the daily puppet shows captured young and old alike. There was Bunin's *Foodini*, Buffalo Bob Smith with *Howdy Doody,* and Burr Tillstrom's award-winning *Kukla, Fran and Ollie*. Topo Gigio, the little Italian Mouse, created a sensation as an infrequent guest on the Ed Sullivan Show. Both Captain Kangaroo and Fred Rogers have mixed people and puppets on their children's television programs. Jim Henson's Muppets have created the New Wave for TV, which is to say that Kermit and Co. have made a big splash in the big time.

On rare occasions Hollywood films a story about puppets and puppeteers. *I Am Suzanne* was the first and featured the Yale Puppeteers. A film adaptation of Margery Sharp's novel *Britannia Mews* came years later, with Dana

Andrews and Maureen O'Hara. Bil Baird's puppets had a sequence in *The Sound of Music*. One of the most unusual puppet success stories concerns the M-G-M film *Lili*, which starred Leslie Caron, Mel Ferrer, Zsa Zsa Gabor, and Jean Pierre Aumont. The puppeteers behind the scenes were Paul Walton, Michael O'Rourke, Wolo, and myself. The basis for the film was a Paul Gallico short story that had appeared in a national magazine. Helen Deutsch did the screen adaptation, and after the film was released Paul Gallico's expanded version came out as a novel, *The Love of Seven Dolls*. After a respectful lull, David Merrick produced a Broadway musical version titled *Carnival*. Tom Tichenor's puppets were featured in it.

Not every puppet could be a star of stage, screen, radio, and television, so others worked as sales demonstrators, educators, and propagandists. A finger puppet walking is the slogan for the Yellow Pages phone directory. Other types of figures have extolled the merits of foundation garments, bathing suits, distillery products, cosmetics, tractor tires, and bank marketing plans. Puppets have held the crowds at industrial shows, trade association meetings, and major department stores. The Higbee Company of Cleveland, Ohio, has presented puppets in its store windows and at various interior locations during seasonal sales promotions. Designer Wally Gbur of Higbee's creates a special puppet stage for each event to tie in with the special theme. Puppets also scurried to the suburbs to greet the crowds at the new shopping malls.

Pinocchio tried to avoid school, but his American counterparts are firmly entrenched in the system starting with kindergarten and moving on up. A hand puppet may serve as an alter ego for the classroom teacher in presenting new material, or a class may build puppets and put on a show to explore a unit on social studies or language arts. Several Ph.D.'s have been granted for dissertation on the puppet theatre, the most recent to Tamara Hunt at The University of Hawaii for a study of the history and influence of Tony Sarg. The fol-

Burr Tillstrom with Kukla and Ollie.

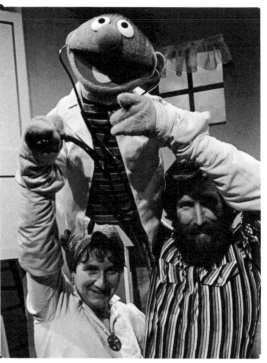

Jane and Jim Henson with Ernie.

Bert and Ernie in Ice Follies.

Leslie Caron, star of Lili, *with Carrot Top and Manipulator George Latshaw. Puppet by Walton and O'Rourke.*

Mervin Mouse at Higbee's "Christmas in the Country." Stage design by Wally Gbur.

The Handley & Miller, Inc., puppet booth at the Bank Marketing Association in Las Vegas, Nevada.

lowing theatre departments have had a long-standing commitment to advanced puppet instruction:

The University of Washington—Aurora Valentinetti

The University of California at Los Angeles —Melvyn B. Helstein

The University of Connecticut—Frank Ballard

Volunteer groups have adopted the puppet as their special educational messenger. For many years, The Association of Junior Leagues provided the services of two national consultants, Alfred Wallace and Jean Starr Wiksell, to assist member groups in preparing productions that were trouped without charge to community schools. In many cities the Dental Wives Auxiliaries use marionettes to promote good tooth care. The A.A.U.W., Elyria Branch, dramatized an ecology theme to show schoolchildren what they could do to help preserve energy and resources. The McDowell Puppeteers, a senior citizens group sponsored by the Columbus (Ohio) Recreation Department, is composed of women in their sixties and seventies. They stay young by playing to young people, and they set a lively example for other oldsters when they play the nursing-home circuit. Concentrating on a performance helps to take their minds off their ailments, they report.

Probably the most urgent and moving demonstration of the puppet speaking to society was Peter Schumann's Bread and Puppet Theatre. There was a medieval simplicity about this group's approach to street theatre, using grotesque superpuppets and masks to protest the war in Vietnam. Their parades and parables conjured up the ancient rites of using the puppet to personify forces threatening the tribe. Religious educators are also using the puppet to bring "life" and meaning to church school programs.

Puppets, old and new, domestic and foreign, are preserved in a number of public and private collections in the United States. They have been the subject of major exhibitions in Chicago, Detroit, Los Angeles, and New York City, not once, but several times. The city of Munich, Germany, has one of the most comprehensive collections in the world. A Puppet Museum is an adjunct of Sergei Obraztsov's theatre in Moscow.

Symphony orchestras have invited puppets to share the concert stage for young people's concerts (and sometimes for adults!). Llords International (Daniel Llords) and Pickwick Puppets (Ken Moses) are two who specialize in this type of performance. Poko Puppets (Virginia Lloyd-Davies and Larry Engler) created the Benny Goodman Quartet for the N.Y. Jazz Museum's "Jazz Puppet Show." Nancy Staub, director of the Puppet Playhouse in New Orleans, has had such success in this field that she was invited to participate with the composer in creating a new work for puppets and orchestra.

The market for hand puppets and marionettes has grown since the Victorian era when Pollock's Toy Theatres (Penny Plain, Two Pence Coloured) brought a touch of drama to the home. Helen Haiman Joseph's Playfellow Marionettes and the Hamburg Puppet Guild's ready-to-assemble kits were among the first in the U.S. market. Virginia Austin Curtis' superbly crafted "Clippo" the clown launched many a budding string puppeteer. In her stage act, Mrs. Curtis manipulated a three-foot-tall marionette of Clippo, who, in turn, worked a smaller one-foot-tall version of Clippo. The sight of one marionette manipulating another marionette never failed to produce amazement and applause. Hazelle Rollins was a leading manufacturer of marionettes and hand puppets for more than twenty-five years, attaining the widest distribution of any American company. Fairy tale characters were grouped by plays they could perform together, and a script was included with every purchase. For variety, toy shops offered imports: The Pelham Puppets from England, the furry Steiff hand-puppet animals from Germany, the droll crocheted puppets from Taiwan, the elegant horse marionettes from Burma, string puppets in som-

PHOTO: ARTHUR W. TONG

PHOTO: JOSEPH KLIMA, JR.

Babar, *with the New Orleans Philharmonic Symphony Orchestra and narrator. Production by Puppet Playhouse, directed by Nancy Staub.*

Till Eulenspiegel, *by Richard Strauss. A Detroit Institute of Arts production with the Detroit Symphony. Designed and directed by George Latshaw.*

COURTESY DANIEL LLORDS

Minuet in Pink, *a concert selection by Llords' "INTERNATIONAL."*

Petrouchka and the Mice, from Petrouchka *by Igor Stravinsky. Produced by Frank Ballard, Department of Dramatic Arts, University of Connecticut.*

breros from Mexico. Jim Henson's *Sesame Street* characters are marketed in many forms, as dolls, puppets, paper figures, punch-out-and-put-together toys, picture books, and magazines.

Puppets provide a gentle way of hiding oneself—the ultimate disguise—so they are well suited to act as go-betweens in a communication between therapist and patient. Obviously one cannot blame a person for what a hand puppet might say or do spontaneously, so it serves as a very liberating device for the subject, and as a very informative tool for the psychologist-observer trained in interpreting such matters. A few children's hospitals are using simple hand puppets to present pre-surgery playlets to their young patients. Puppets of a doctor, nurse, and child act out the preparation for the operation and the recovery when it is over. After seeing the play, children are encouraged to ask questions and to express any fears they may hold. The puppet example can lessen the fear of the unknown. If the puppet, which is much smaller than the child, has courage to face the situation, the child may be encouraged to try the same behavior.

Today the puppet is reaching more people and serving more needs than ever before in its history—and it survives because it serves.

How would you describe a puppeteer? Who is s/he? What does s/he do? What is the difference between an actor and a puppeteer? Where does the ventriloquist fit in?

Compare these definitions.

> **ac-tor** (ak′ tər), n.   1. one who represents fictitious or historical characters in a play, motion picture, broadcast, etc.   2. one who acts, doer.
> **pup-pe-teer** (pup′ə-ti′r), n.   a person who operates, designs, or costumes puppets, or produces puppet shows.
> **ven-tril-o-quist** (ven-tril′ə-kwist), n.   a person who practices ventriloquism (speaking in such a way that the voice seems to come from some other source than the speaker); specifically, an entertainer who uses ventriloquism to carry on a pretended conversation with a large puppet, or dummy.

The actor, puppeteer, and ventriloquist have similar functions. Each one assumes a role to perform before an audience, but there is a world of difference in their purpose, preparation, and performance.

Actors work in full view of the audience using their own physical and vocal skills. Puppeteers do just the opposite. They hide from the audience and substitute bodies (the puppets) and sometimes voices that are not their own. The visible ventriloquist, controlling the visible dummy, combines elements of each approach.

Being invisible is the distinctive trademark of most puppeteers. In performance they are out of sight, so it is difficult to identify who they are or what they do. We tend to think of anyone who works backstage as a part of the crew—the technicians, electricians, stagehands, and wardrobe and prop people who are necessary to the effective running of the show, but who are not included in the curtain calls. Suc-

cessful puppeteers make us forget their presence, and we applaud the puppets as the performers we have seen.

It is not modesty that makes a puppeteer divert attention from himself. If we think of him as a magician, the need for mystery makes sense. When it is time to go on stage, he disappears. To take his place, he conjures up a whole array of things. These things can move; they speak; they seem to be alive. The conjurer, transformed, leaves not a trace of who he was or where he went. Reality recedes. Amazing images appear. It is like discovering intelligent, English-speaking life from another planet. The puppet stage becomes a Parable or Fable for Earthlings.

Puppeteers introduce a totally new dimension to the performing arts by designing and creating a world of their own in which animated objects are the actors. The result is a unique, nonhuman theatre. It is sometimes a reminder or reflection of the living stage, but it can never be a reproduction of it, because it does not start with the same reality—the visible human actor. Puppeteers change the rules by changing the players; consequently they end up in a class by themselves. Their work is considered adjacent to, but always apart from, the other fields of performance.

This performance isolation is both a source of power and a problem for the puppeteer. The problem is in being recognized. The power is in being liberated from human, physical limitations. The customary casting requirements of "looking the part" or being the right "type" do not apply to puppeteers. They manufacture whatever appearance the role requires, be it tall or short, fat or thin, handsome or ugly, male or female. Puppeteers can project an "image" that is perfect for the part regardless of their own physical dimensions or condition. Puppeteers do not have to be able to stand on their hands, turn cartwheels, dance, fence, or juggle, but they delight in making their puppets do these things. All energy and action are channeled into the figures being manipulated; the movements of the puppeteer at work seem oddly detached and restrained in comparison with the lively action of the puppet.

Voices, too, can be manufactured for the puppeteer. In the Sicilian theatre the lines are spoken by offstage readers. The physical demands of handling the 50- to 75-pound rod puppets require this practical division of labor. One part of the team supplies the dramatic voice, the other supplies the lusty action. In the Japanese theatre, the chanter or *joruri* is an artist in his own right. The operatic nature of the speech and sound effects requires intensive training for the men or women who speak the narrative passages and all character voices in a scene. The solo chanter follows a written text to samisen accompaniment and sets the pace for the manipulators of the dolls. The modern puppeteer may substitute a taped voice sound track for the live voices. Those who prefer the taped playback feel that the consistent vocal performance level frees them to concentrate all attention on the manipulation. The Kappa-Za Troupe of Japan is able to perform in the language of the tour country by piping the local language to the audience, while receivers on the puppeteers' costumes are receiving the dialogue track in Japanese. In the United States puppet operas have been staged as elaborate record pantomimes with classical music. Recordings of the world's great orchestras and voices supply the sound while the visual elements are mimed by puppets. A backstage prompter, following the score and libretto, coaches the unseen manipulators by whispering stage directions during the performance in the best opera tradition.

The ventriloquist is really a puppeteer who enjoys working out in the open to get double exposure. In the comedy team of the vent person and the dummy, two contrasting personalities emerge. The human is usually low-key and straightforward, whereas the puppet is sassy, impudent, and irrepressible. It takes great skill and concentration to maintain two distinctly separate roles in a rapid crossfire of repartee. Imagine keeping your mouth shut and listening intently to conceal the fact that you are speaking the outrageous lines you are listening to. It is a mind-boggling feat of misdirection and enough to split the ego clean in two. Of course humans are the butt of the jokes. The dummy makes all the smart remarks, wisecracks, and "mow 'em down" tag lines. The ventriloquist tends to be overshadowed, for the public is such a pushover for a puppet with pizzazz that it is the dummy who turns out to be the star and steals the show.

Whether it was the example of the ventriloquist working out in the open, or simply an urgent need to be seen on stage, variety and nightclub performers created a sensation in the 1930's by presenting marionettes without masking. The puppeteer, working in full view of the audience, was an integral and visual part of the act. The audience loved the style, and it solved a number of problems for the performer. It was a quick way to reduce the amount of equipment to be transported and set up; it was a better way to share the spotlight and the applause; and it was a surefire way to capture a sophisticated adult audience by letting them see who was doing it and how it was done. People who had seen everything felt they had stumbled onto a secret side of show biz. It had the suspense of a sporting event. Audiences could watch the puppet; they could watch the puppeteer; they could try to second-guess the next move. A variety act, running 12 to 20 minutes, would feature trick figures, dancers, and maybe a "celebrity" or two on strings. The striptease, come-apart skeleton, skater, ballerina, and juggler were

Walton (right) and O'Rourke, with Cleo.

Jim Gamble and special friends.

Jay Marshall and Lefty.

Erica Melchior marionettes.

standard bits. Usually talk pieces were not included, although the puppeteer might MC to bridge the routines.

In the theatre, a solo performance by an actor or actress is noteworthy by its rarity. Cornelia Otis Skinner and Ruth Draper were famous for their one-woman shows. More recently Hal Holbrook, James Whitmore, and Henry Fonda have turned their one-man shows into personal tours de force. To the puppeteer, however, working alone is a way of life. He or she may be a soloist, not from any star status, but from necessity. Puppetry seems to attract persons who enjoy the "jack of all trades" aspect of the field, and the decision to work alone may be economic, artistic, or personal.

OVERVIEW

The actor is one person playing one role at a time. His primary business is to act—usually in the company of other actors. The ventriloquist takes on two roles simultaneously, alternating between a person role and a dummy character—in effect, playing a duet with himself. The puppeteer stretches even further to assume multiple identities, in addition to doing all the technical phases of production. An actor who enjoys being a ham is no match for the puppeteer who wants to be the whole hog.

These are some of the reasons for being a puppeteer:

Based on Appearance

1) The puppet provides the "ideal" appearance for a role; it projects the visual "essence" of the character.

2) A puppet can make you appear to be smaller than human size—a dwarf, an elf, a gnome, a fairy, a troll, a goblin, a leprechaun.

3) A puppet allows you to appear to be larger than life—a giant, a monster, an ogre, a dragon, a towering grotesque.

4) A puppet can be a caricature, grotesque or amusing. An extreme distortion of proportions is possible.

5) A puppet can be an inanimate object or even an abstract shape that moves. A variety of nonhuman forms can spring to life to become the players.

Based on Action

6) The puppet is an alternate anatomy for acting and does not have to be constructed following the human skeletal structure and jointing system. The design, construction, and substance of the puppet can allow it to move in novel and wondrous ways.

7) Some puppets can say "Good-bye Gravity." They can float, rise, fly, or walk on air, defying the natural laws that keep the actor earthbound.

8) Puppets can play tricks with time— slow motion on the ground, a languid leap in the air, and what goes up can take its own sweet time coming down. A puppet can streak across the scene with almost blurred speed.

Based on Personal Choice

9) The puppet allows one person to play two roles at once or even all the roles in a production. Male and female roles can be played by the same person.

10) The puppeteer can be the external observer of his own performance as it is happening.

11) The puppet promises the "fountain of youth" to the puppeteer, for its form is frozen in time from the moment of creation. The puppeteer may wrinkle and gray, but there are no telltale signs in the puppet character that the audience sees. The "ideal" image can last a lifetime.

12) The puppet is a monument to immortality, for it survives the death of its creator and is a memorial to the life that animated it. No other performing art can preserve the exact "presence" that the audience knew, in this way.

13) The puppeteer can control all facets of

production, from conception to curtain call. In the one-person show, there is no need for the cooperation and compromise that occurs when many departments collaborate on a theatrical venture. All these talents (and limitations) are contained in one person, who must answer to no one else. Playing with puppets is a form of playing god of all creation.

The complexity of the puppeteer might be summed up this way. S/he is a special kind of actor-technician who channels performance through a foreign body, using illusion, exhibition, and animation, to achieve the ultimate disguise. These disguises can protect the physical identity of the creator, while revealing many facets of the personality.

The differences between the actor and the puppeteer are more apparent when comparing their methods of preparation and performance.

PREPARATION

Actor

Tryouts: Open call

Casting: Director's Choice

Rehearsal Period:
Blocking
Lines and business
Characterization
Ensemble playing
Pace, mood, build
(Actor attends rehearsals in work clothes.)

Tech Rehearsals:
Costume parade, focus lights, check makeups, run sound and light cues. Rehearse scene shifts.

Dress Rehearsals:
All performance conditions, with the possibility of preview audiences before opening.

Puppeteer
(One-person show)

Tryouts: None

Casting: Self-select

Construction Period:
Set script or action outline
Design and build puppets
Construct sets & props
Finish costumes
Paint on makeup, add wigs
Record music, sound effects
(and voice track, if used)

Rehearsal Period:
Blocking on the set

(The puppet arrives at a first reading in dress-rehearsal readiness of full costume and makeup.)
Lines and business
Voice and movement characterization.

Tech Rehearsals:
An ongoing condition of rehearsals. Set sound and light cues.

Dress Rehearsals:
With or without a critical eye out front in the director's role.
Test audience of family or friends.

PERFORMANCE

Actor	*Puppeteer*
Actor in costume and makeup visible to audience.	Puppeteer backstage and unseen by audience.
Actor has some visual awareness of audience, plus audible responses heard.	Puppeteer cannot see audience and must rely wholly on sound clues for feedback.
Actor to audience—direct contact.	Puppeteer to puppet; puppet to audience—indirect contact.
Full use of physical and vocal skills.	Puppeteer's movements confined to those that move the puppet effectively.
Onstage only when his/her role requires it.	Onstage for entire performance, playing all the roles.
No technical responsibilities except for costume, makeup, and hand props to be carried on and off.	All technical responsibilities, from raising curtain, dimming lights, shifting set pieces, working sound cues, etc.
Interacts with other players.	Interacts with self.
Concentrating on a role, actor does not drop out of character to check performance while on stage.	Able to monitor the performance, as the actor saying the lines, the director controlling the movement, and as an audience to his own work. S/he is a triple track player.

Applause for the Actors	*Applause for the Puppets*
Backstage—recognition and rejoicing.	Backstage—visitors often bypass the puppeteer for a closer look at the puppets, sets, stage etc., because these are the elements they have seen.
May enjoy a long run in a permanent theatre.	Generally a one-night stand, with portable puppet stage and puppets to be packed, loaded into vehicle, and moved on.

Finally we must consider the recognition and rewards for the puppeteer, as well as the attitudes theatre people and the public have toward them and their work.

It has been disappointing to discover that many young actors reject the idea of performing with puppets. For them, being seen by the audience is part of the thrill and satisfaction of acting. They will wear any outrageous costume, suffer through any weird makeup, endure any contortions to move—as long as they are visible to the public. They would balk at wearing a mask "because you wouldn't be able to see my face!"—and, of course, the puppet would eliminate the perception of the body as well. For an actor, this would be "nowhere." I suspect that an actor would prefer to play the corpse in the second act rather than submit to having a puppet stand-in on stage. Actors may feel that a puppeteer is synonymous with being anonymous, and it is true that one dictionary on my shelf does not even list the word "puppeteer" although "puppet" is defined. This would confirm the actors' suspicions that recognition in puppetry is minimal, being directed toward the object rather than the person. Puppets have no life without actors, but actors can certainly live without puppets. They look at the puppet as a step down, whereas the non-actor or amateur looks on the puppet as a step up. The puppet gives them the visible signs of "acting" (costume, makeup, character) that the nonprofessional would not put on if exposed to view. The puppet seems so performance-ready that it invites assistance from all comers.

Occasionally a producer for films or television will decide to eliminate the high cost of humans by "hiring" puppets, reasoning that costs can be scaled downward as the size of the performers, sets, costumes, etc., decreases. Half the size at half the price, or "Puppets will work cheap" as the saying goes. The initial shock comes in discovering the time it takes to construct replacements for the actors, and the second one is the disappointment that marionettes are not really miniature actors who can do anything required impromptu on the set. There is no substitute for the live actor, and none for the puppet, but both must be given script and style appropriate to their special skills. At least one producer turned to puppet production to avoid the friction of temperament, personalities, and egos of the live talent. "Puppets will do what they are told and can't talk back" is an old joke. In this delusion, puppeteers are tolerated as the flunkies or bodyguards who hang around with the puppets, without being recognized as having a hand in the artistry and the action.

In the United States puppets and children are paired in the public mind. The combination is natural, since imagination and fantasy are a part of childhood play; children's literature is filled with adventures in nonreal worlds; and puppets are a partial fulfillment of childhood dreams and wishes.

Watch children at play with their toys—the huggable teddy bears, the much-loved dolls, the floppy clowns, and the frazzled, furry puppy dogs. Children are able to give and receive affection from inanimate objects. The puppet is a logical extension of this pretending.

Children's literature abounds with fanciful images that the puppets can play to perfection. Elves and leprechauns, monsters, giants, and dragons are the special province of the puppet world. Human actors trying to enact the wee folk are often embarrassing as they prance around trying to imitate pixies. It takes more than leotards and a pointed cap to convert these oversize, overweight oafs into anything more than caricatures. Even Peter Pan has to be hoisted in the manner of a marionette in order to fly to Never Never Land. The children's theatre producers could mix puppets and people to create more entrancing stage illusions than are currently being seen. The theatre at Carnegie Tech produced *Midsummer Night's Dream* twice using that technique.

The puppet as a partial promise of a world beyond reality holds special appeal to children. Setting aside wishes and dreams for the obviously fantastic is seen as a mark of maturity, and yet the urge to find something more lingers on in the recurring interest in UFO's, Big Foot, Martians, the Abominable Snowman, and the Loch Ness monster. Adults are intrigued but apt to be humorously skeptical about such possibilities. Adult fantasy tends to be centered on sex and science fiction, and there are puppeteers who have done interesting work in each area.

Post-performance treatment of the actor is better than that accorded the puppeteer. Backstage visitors at a puppet show are notorious pinchers and feelers. They rap on heads to test construction materials; they squeeze bodies to find out what is inside; and they lift skirts to see how the legs are attached to the marionette body. One touring company thwarted the curious by putting bloomers on all the ladies in the cast. A less inhibited nightclub puppeteer gave Peeping Toms a jolt by fashioning the anatomically correct details to greet the patrons who were looking where they should not have been. Misguided fans expect to find the secret of performance in the "craft" of puppetry—the construction or materials—and they ignore the artistry of the animator who made them live.

I remember a delightful performance of *St. George and the Dragon,* presented by "Kukla, Fran and Ollie" at a national festival of the Puppeteers of America. Almost before the final applause died down, the puppeteers stormed the stage to express their enthusiasm. A crowd gathered around Fran Allison, and the rest headed straight for the puppet booth, only to find it completely empty. The Kuklapolitans had been whisked away. The puppeteers were nonplussed. They had come to congratulate Kukla, Ollie, Beulah Witch, et al, and their favorites had fled. Slowly the dawn began to break, as people turned around to give Burr Tillstrom the recognition he richly deserved.

An artist compels us to believe, in spite of knowing how it is done. Being a puppeteer is not everyone's cup of tea, and we should be grateful to those who do it well, for they achieve the ultimate disguise.

Chapter III

ACTOR INTO ANIMATOR

To help others discover what it feels like to be a puppeteer, I have designed a sequence of "exercises" to be used in a workshop situation. *Each exercise poses a problem unique to the puppeteer-performer.* Workshop participants are asked to come up with solutions to these problems. As they generate information with each solution, they are advanced to another problem until a concept of the puppeteer emerges at the end.

This fun-and-games approach to learning is also known as "experiential education." The premise is that every person has the skills to solve problems if given the challenge and opportunity; and that it is more exciting for the students to learn by experiencing than by teacher-tell. The goal is to develop an independent student who can set new problems and solve them as part of a lifelong learning process. This is the philosophy behind creative drama, improvisation, theatre games, exercises, simulation games, and learning labs.

To set up the exercises we need an even-numbered group of participants, 12 to 16 persons; a group leader (also known as a trainer or facilitator) who is skilled in handling the group process; and a large room with enough open space for the participants to move freely.

PROCEDURE

1) The leader presents the exercise outlining the problem and specifies how it is to be carried out: by the total group responding simultaneously; by individual response; by two persons working together as partners; or by teams of a designated number.

The leader establishes the ground rules for these exercises: there is no "right" or "wrong" way to do them. The solutions are to come from the natural, spontaneous, intuitive response that each person has to the material, and that will produce a variety of possible solutions.

2) Allow an adequate time to prepare each exercise.

3) Presentation of the exercise to the total group, which is the means of sharing the solutions. We learn from our own experience; we can also learn from the experience of others. The group can generate a lot of information in a short time.

4) Some exercises call for a "reflection" period, or a response from the observers of a presentation. The leader must handle this carefully, so that it stays a "reflection" of what was seen and not a critique of what was "good" or "bad" in the presentation. The performers need to know what the audience saw in order to make their own evaluation of what communicated and what did not. They should be free to revise their solution or come up with another, if they feel it necessary. A person who fails may not want to continue the experiment, but a person who has learned something is already moving forward. A leader is present to keep the focus on the "learning" of the group.

FIRST SERIES

Everyone works simultaneously but independently. There are no observers.

Exercise #1—Feel and Freeze

This is similar to the children's game of "Statues." Each person should have enough space to move freely without touching the next person. Stand with feet a comfortable distance apart for balance, but do not move out of position during the exercise. Go through random motions of swinging, bending, twisting, reaching, using free movement of arms, torso, and knees. When a descriptive word is called out by the leader, move into a posture which represents that word to you and freeze. Hold that pose until the leader says, "Move." Swing freely again until another word is called, pose, freeze, and repeat.

LAZY—Freeze—Move
EXUBERANT—Freeze—Move
PAINED—Freeze—Move
REVERENT—Freeze—Move
DEFIANT—Freeze—Move and relax.

Exercise #2—Repeat

This time take a basic position with feet apart, body leaning forward slightly, head looking down at the floor, arms at sides, bent at elbow, with hands held out in front at waist level. This is the basic position for all random movement and freeze positions.

SORROW—Freeze—Move
FRENZY—Freeze—Move
HATE—Freeze—Move
SURPRISE—Freeze—Move
PASSION—Freeze—Move and relax.

Exercise #3—Variation—Repeat

This time assume a position with both hands held straight overhead. Without moving the arms from their upright position, go through random movement, changing what you can of face, body, legs, fingers, and hands. Arms remain aloft through every descriptive word, pose, and freeze.

TIRED—Freeze—Move
ANGRY—Freeze—Move

LOVE—Freeze—Move
FEAR—Freeze—Move
FROLIC—Freeze—Move and relax.

Reflection—How did you feel about doing these movements? In which position were you most free? In which were you most confined? What did you need for the fullest expression of each descriptive pose? How did you adapt to the fixed positions in Exercises #2 and #3?

The first exercise explored the actor's freedom to move body and limbs in space. The second exercise simulated the position of a string puppeteer, and the third demonstrated the problems of the hand puppeteer working overhead.

Exercise #4—Two-sided Variation

This time we shall get a taste of what it feels like to handle two hand puppets in the overhead position. Return to the start of Exercise #3. Pretend that your right arm and your left arm are independent of each other. When the leader calls out the first word, assume the descriptive pose with your right arm only. Hold that position. When the leader calls out the second word, move into that pose with the left arm only. At the cue to "relax," drop both poses, but not both arms. Do this for each set of words called, and watch each arm pose as you do it to see if the left hand "responds" to the right hand's pose.

TIRED—Freeze	ALERT—Freeze—Relax
ANGRY—Freeze	PEACEFUL—Freeze—Relax
LOVE—Freeze	EXPLODE—Freeze—Relax
FEAR—Freeze	BRAVE—Freeze—Relax
LOOSE—Freeze	RIGID—Freeze—Relax and hands down.

This quick introduction to what happens to the puppeteer's body position during performance may require a pause for comments and reactions from the group. The leader should encourage the group to share any feelings or discoveries after each exercise.

It is not possible to do all the exercises in this chapter during one class period, nor is it desirable to work that fast. There must be some time to assimilate and absorb the information, and, in fact, the completion of the entire set may take as much as a week. In the case of outside assignments some planning time should be allowed during the regular meeting. Presentations that are prepared outside of class and brought in usually take one full session to share, with guided reflection periods.

SECOND SERIES

Divide the group into two teams (or self-select), with half the group in each team. One group performs, the other observes; then reverse.

Exercise #5—Group Shape

This exercise is an assemblage or add-on. One person starts the shape by assuming a position in the staging area. This person explores the space and strikes a position that will start the design. A second person volunteers to join on, and after considering the possibilities assumes a position that will extend, enhance, complement, counteract, or balance the shape established by the first person. Each member of the team follows in turn, joining on to any portion of the shape, until all members are a part of the group shape.

Reflection: (For participants) How did you decide when and where to add on? (For observers) What did you see happening to the form as it grew?

Repeat exercise, trading teams. Repeat reflection.

Exercise #6—Abstract Animated Sculpture

Have the group count off by two's to form two new working units.

Abstract sculpture is nonrepresentational,

and its forms use both positive and negative space. Motion is sometimes added, using air currents, wind, running water, or motors. Each team is to find a work space and take some time to prepare an abstract, animated sculpture using only themselves as the building elements. The finished sculpture should contain no "human" elements, that is, no charging horses, no historic monuments. The sculpture must include every member of the team in the finished product, and it must move. When the teams have prepared their sculptures (5 to 10 minutes), they are to return to the central area. Each team presents its sculpture in the center of the room, so that the observers are free to move around all sides as if viewing it in a gallery.

Reflection: (For the sculptors) What helped the form to develop? How did the group make decisions? Did you talk it through or actively experiment? Was there shared leadership in the group? (For the observers) What form did you see? By what means was it animated? What textures and materials did it suggest?

Exercise #7—Make a Machine

Leader divides group into two new teams.

Using arms, legs, and bodies of the group as the building tools, construct a workable machine that can perform a service or manufacture a product. It can be a household appliance, a factory assembly line, a farm machine, or whatever the group wishes. The problem in the exercise is to create the machine so clearly that the audience can recognize it as one they know. This is not a guessing game or charade, but an exercise in communication. Each team should retire to a separate space to prepare (10 to 15 minutes). Presentation of the machines.

Reflection: What did you see? What clues did you have to the function/use of this machine? What signals made the presentation clear to you?

Examples: A number of groups have made

washing machines, blenders, typewriters, lawn-mowers, wheat harvesters, and electric toasters. One group concocted a player piano. Although the leader does not specify sound, a group is permitted to use sound effects if their team requests this right.

Exercise #8—The Creation of a World

Regroup into two or three new teams.
Each group is to create a world in which an inaminate object comes to life for the first time. This world does not contain people. The group should select an object (or several of the same) that does not live or move. What brings it to life? How does it move? What happens then? Give time for preparation. All members must be involved in the presentation.

Reflection: What did you see? What came to life? What made the action clear?

Example: At the Eugene O'Neill Memorial Theatre Institute, one of my groups solved this problem by bringing popcorn to life. They created the pan, the kernels, the shaking process, the heating up, the popping up and down, and finally the whole group explosion into life.

This ends the first segment. It would be a good time to reflect on the usefulness of group activity and on the visual illusions that have been created without the use of props or objects. What principles of animation has the group discovered that would be useful to a puppeteer? The leader should make sure that the basic ground rules are being observed, so that all members feel involved and contribute to the problem-solving process. It is important to restate the value of each member's contribution to the work of the entire group. If one participant has been dominating the group activity by making all the decisions, the leader should intervene as it occurs.

It is easier to build trust and confidence in members of a new group by starting with non-verbal exercises, which keep the focus on the group and not on the individual. By this time participants should have no hesitation about using their bodies in varied ways to create the necessary effects. These demonstrations should

help to expand the concept of puppetry from visions of it as a small-scale, small-number activity to large-scale, large-effects possibilities. New views of puppet theatre performance should be generating in the group.

THIRD SERIES

Exercise #9—An Outside Assignment: Create a Ritual

Divide into teams of 6 to 8. Select a society of a simple or primitive nature. The character range can be high priest, shaman, witch doctor, voodoo maker, wizard, etc. The central character probably has assistants and subjects in the performance of the ritual. Decide upon the society and create a ritual in which an inanimate object moves as the central act of magic in the piece. Characterize the magician or assistant and show the effect of the magic on the beholders. No trick effects such as flash powder, flash paper, etc., may be used. The magic must be under human control, but undetected. Allow time to assemble props and sound effects. (Candles, incense, etc., are allowable.) In each ritual there will be observers within the scene as well as the audience of observers. In this exercise time should be set aside to plan and rehearse the ritual. It is important that these rehearsals take place away from the other team(s) so that the effect will be fresh. For the rehearsal assemble the props, prepare the environment, and run through the roles and effects. Present each ritual and allow time for reflection before moving on to the next ritual.

Reflection: What was the magic you saw? Was it hidden from the beholders? What were its effects? Can you tell why it had these effects?

Usually the presentation of the rituals should provide a session in itself. The response is such that it would be an intrusion to introduce a new aspect at this point. Let the observers savor what they saw. An understanding of the root beginnings they have made toward animating the inanimate will begin to seep into their consciousness. For some, the implications are awesome.

SERIES FOUR

Exercise #10—Simple Communication Using Hand Signals Only

The leader should demonstrate some commonly accepted hand signals that we use to communicate nonverbally with each other. These include the peace sign, the hitchhiker's sign with a thumb, the waggling finger for "no, no, no," and the gesture "Come here" with index finger or hand.

Hand signals are a shorthand form of nonverbal communication. What other signals can group members think of? Allow some time to try them together.

Divide the group into teams of two.

Working with a partner, each member should develop a communication with the other person using hand signals only. Do not discuss what you are going to say before you try it. One partner can leap in and start the communication with a signal and the other person must respond to the signal given—react to it. The signals should continue until the partners have come to the end of the communication. Then each team can share its hand-signal communication with the group.

Reflection for Group: Did you find it easy or difficult to convey all the meaning you wished using the hands only? If the observers were not able to follow the hand signals, where did they look for clues? Did they check faces, or body language?

Note: A puppeteer often uses this form of isolating a portion of his body to animate a puppet. If the meaning is not clear in the portion the audience can see, the puppet will not communicate. Despite the puppeteer's facial expression and body language backstage, the audience will understand only what is visible to it.

Exercise #11—Repeat—with Masking so Only Hands Are Visible

Use a blanket held by two sides, a blackboard, or other simple masking to hide the performers so that their faces and bodies cannot be seen. Paired with new partners, the two-member teams should develop hand communications and share these communications with the whole group, allowing only their hands to show above the masking. It should be easier to follow the communication this time, since the puppeteers will be trying the exercise for the second time and the masking provides a barrier so that only the essential information is transmitted. The awareness that the audience cannot see anything but hands will help performers to avoid aimless pantomime and get down to simple signal language. After all teams have shared the communications, take time for a general reflection.

Reflection: How was this sequence different from the last one? What made it that way?

Exercise #12—Isolation Exercise with Feet Visible

Regroup with new partners. This time agree in advance on the character that each partner will play, but show the action only with the portion of the leg from the shinbone down, using ankles and feet. Prepare the communication with these instruments and then share them. Again, the communication is nonverbal. Use no words, but only the action of legs and feet. Some people may think to work in socks or bare feet to delineate characterization or enhance "expressiveness." Since the instructions did not limit that possibility, it is permissible, but the leader should allow teams to discover this and not suggest it. The purpose of the exercise is to explore isolation or communication through isolated elements—which may seem limited at first—and to focus all communication to take place through them.

Reflection: What characters did you see? What did they do?

Exercise #13—Use of Hands to Create Illusions

In Exercises #10 and #11, the hands were used in an everyday way so that we perceived hands in action doing what hands can do to communicate. This time, regrouped and paired

PHOTO: LLOYD WITTER

Hand in Glove, *a Bird on the Hand Beats the Bush. George Latshaw Puppets.*

with a new partner, use fingers, hands, arms to make us see something else. Help the observers to see some living thing from the earth, the sky, or the sea, and under the earth. As options, each partner can create one thing using one or both hands or both partners together can combine all elements to create a single effect. These may be separate living things or they may interact. Some of the things I have seen created are: birds, spiders, rabbits, flowers growing out of the ground, raindrops, Venus's flytrap, snakes, snails, turtles, baby bird mouths in a nest, turkey, swan, and butterfly. If the group seems to have a number of creatures from each of the locales, they might be regrouped by land, sea, and air and given the task of interrelating the creatures they have created.

Yves Joly, a contemporary French puppeteer, should be credited with this breakthrough of using hands alone. It was revolu-tionary to see that illusions could be created without any "costumes" (i.e., puppets). His original hand ballets have influenced the entire world of modern puppetry. The puppeteer can animate the images he envisions by a creative use of his own anatomy.

SERIES FIVE

Exercise #14—Scale Smaller than Human

Regroup into teams of two players each. Each team should think of very small living things or small inanimate objects. One member of the team is to be something small. The other member of the team remains human size and relates to the living thing or the inanimate object and its use. Prepare two different scenes in each team by reversing roles so that each member has an opportunity to be the small thing and the thing of human scale. Share the two scenes with the group. Bouncing a ball and playing croquet are two interesting solutions that have been made to the problem. Some people make the transfer from previous exercises and use an isolated portion to represent the whole—a finger becomes a fountain pen, etc. Others use the actor's means of the total body compressed to the smallest space.

Reflection: Following each team's presentation, discuss what you saw. If observers are not sure, let players try to show or tell in another way. This will sharpen players' ability to show and observers' ability to see.

Exercise #15—Scale Larger than Human

Regroup partners. What are the largest objects, structures, beings, forces you can think of? One member of the team should become the "super size" and the other remain human size and relate to the giant. The team should also reverse roles so that each person gets to play both parts. Prepare, share, reflect.

Reflection: What did you see? What devices helped increase the size (chairs, tables, etc.)? Share feelings about being small or large, and permit members to state their preference for size. Explore other possibilities for solving the problem of size.

Exercise #16—Two-fers—"I'll Be the Body, You Be the Voice"

This exercise requires four players per unit. Two players decide on characters and a situation for a pantomime scene. These two can move but not speak. The other two players provide the voices for the characters who move. The "voices" sit apart from the pantomimists and speak as the actors "mime" the scene. Players doing the mimed action are not to try to lip sync the words, since these will be spontaneous and impromptu, but the basic outline of the dialogue and action are to be worked out in preparation. In this way the actors will have some idea of what the "voices" will be saying. After the first experience the partners should reverse roles so that each person has an opportunity to be an actor and a

voice. These scenes should be shared and time allowed for reflection on each.

Reflection: Did voice and action seem to blend into "one"? Which was easier to do—the movement or the voice? Did you try to establish which half would take the lead—the voice or the actor—or did it just "happen"?

Exercise #17—Present Arms

Regroup into teams of two players. One person provides the face and torso of a figure. The second person, standing behind the first, contributes the arms to go with the first person. The problem is to work out a sequence of action so that the effect is of one body with the arms doing all the action. Standing or sitting positions will be the easiest. Do not attempt to walk or move. Think of action using arms, hands, face, hands relating to face and torso. Reverse the roles and work out new action. Share the solutions with the other teams. Examples of solutions include shaving, toothbrushing, hair-combing, makeup, lipstick, eyelashes, powder, donning glasses, lighting cigarettes, taking something out of pocket and putting it back.

Reflection: Did you see "one" whole person? Did the face and body seem comfortable with what the arms were doing?

SERIES SIX

Exercise #18—Outside Assignment: Create a Paper-bag Mask

Create a mask using a brown paper bag as the base. Do not shorten the bag or cut away anything except eye slits. Create features with Magic Marker or colored construction paper cut out and pasted to the bag. Eye holes or slits for seeing do not have to be the eyes of the mask. They can be the nostrils, mouth, or whatever. The mask may be a primitive tribal mask, an animal, a monster, or anything except a human being. Bring the mask to the next session with a blanket, sheet, throw, or other large fabric covering that can cover the body head-to-toe in soft drapery.

Exercise #19—Moving in the Mask

Give some time for experiment and preparation, then ask each person to move in the mask in a way that seems to match the face on the mask. The person must be wearing the mask during the movement.

Reflection: Was the movement forceful? Was the mask forceful? What is different about wearing a mask—for the wearer? for the watcher?

Before the next exercise, it is helpful to move into a space that has mirrors—dressing room, dance studio—so that each mask-wearer can study the effect of movement by watching the reflecting image of mask and covered body. Videotape equipment can be used, also.

Exercise #20—Mirror Image of the Mask-wearer.

This exercise requires a team of two, with one partner masked, one unmasked. The partners face each other. The unmasked person tries to follow the movement as the masked person takes the lead. The unmasked person must concentrate on all that he/she sees, even to the facial expression on the mask, so that the mask-wearer can have the sense of seeing exactly what is being done. Play this directly with observers watching each unit. The team members should then reverse roles with the same partner.

Reflection: Did the mask-wearer "see" what he/she was doing in the reflected action? Did the observers feel they were seeing mirrored images?

Exercise #21—Echo Image

This exercise requires two-partner teams. One person studies the mask carefully and designs movement for the other partner, the mask-wearer, to follow. The first person makes no more than three moves and then holds or freezes in position. The mask-wearer follows those three moves. The "designer" increases the strength and effectiveness of the mask by

designing three more movements, which the mask-wearer follows. Again, the partners should reverse roles so that each plays "designer" and mask-wearer.

Reflection: (On designing and "scaling up" movement to meet requirements of the mask.) Did the movements grow? Did the movements reflect the character of the mask? Did the mask influence the person's design of movement? Did the person influence the mask?

Exercise #22—Half and Half

This exercise requires new pairs of partners working with the masks. The teams require newspaper or some filler for the bag mask, which is not worn. The mask is attached to a stick, broom handle, or similar object. One corner of the blanket, sheet, or other drapery is attached to the stick at the base of the mask. This hanging forms the "body." One person holds the mask on the stick and uses one corner of the drapery for a hand. The partner holds the waist of the mask holder and holds up the opposite corner of drapery for another

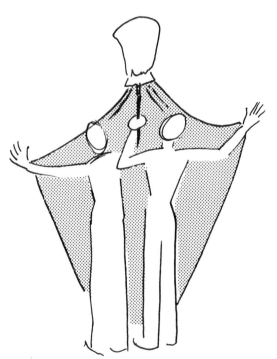

Mask and drapery for two puppeteers.

hand. The mask is held overhead, so drapery partially conceals the bodies of the holders. The two people work together to animate the two arms and head in an action.

Reflection: What were the problems in coordinating the figure? How did each team move to solve these problems?

SERIES SEVEN

Exercise #23—Wrap-up Concept: Newspaper Project
Needed—stacks of newspapers, Sunday comics, etc. Rolls of ½″ masking tape.
The leader should generate input on the various ways in which newspaper might be handled to create form and shape when no tools such as knives, scissors, etc., may be used. For example, newspaper may be rolled, folded, torn, crumpled, curled, stuffed, wadded, or fringed. The leader should suggest that students remember the simple constructions children make of paper such as snowflakes, rings, loops, accordion folds, fans, etc.

PHOTO: ULDIS SAULE

Northwestern University students animate their 6-foot-long newspaper "marionette."

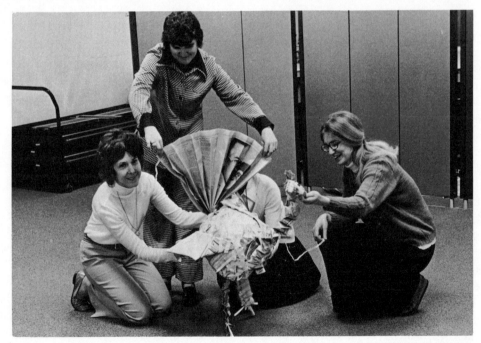

PHOTO: STEVE GRIFFITHS

Johnson County Community College workshop. The theatre is directed by Matthias Campbell III, and George Latshaw is workshop leader. Note the workable tail feathers on the newspaper bird.

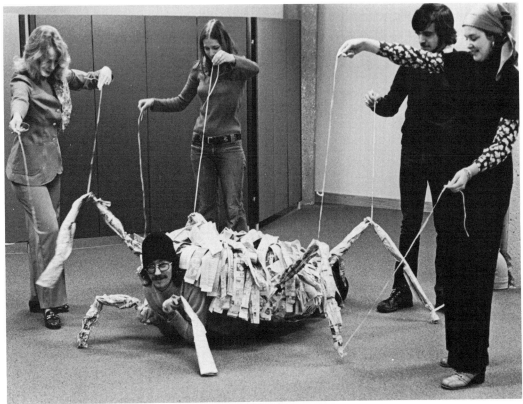

PHOTO: STEVE GRIFFITHS

Johnson County Community College workshop newspaper project. The spider form is animated both from inside and out.

The group is then divided into teams of three or more players and given the following instructions. Using only the newspaper and masking tape, and no tools, construct a figure that can be animated by the number of people who construct it. It can be real or imaginary, but the creature must be brought to life, and it is essential that each person on the team be involved in animating it. The creature should be named, make a sound, and move. Time allowed for completion of the project is 45 minutes to one hour. A fascinating variety of solutions to the total concept of disguise have emerged with different groups. Some build a figure around a person inside and work the external portions. Some work totally outside, using hand grips or direct hand holds to animate the figure. Some have folded masking tape strips together to make "strings" to control the figures. Some have rolled tight cylinders to make rod extensions to control the figure. They have created witches and animals such as an octopus, a crocodile, a bird, an elephant, a dinosaur and a dragon. The great surprise occurred one summer when two boys fulfilled all the requirements of animating what they made. They wadded newspaper into a baseball mitt, a baseball, and a bat and proceeded to pitch and hit.

If it has seemed odd to approach the concept of the puppeteer without using any puppets, I will admit that my bias favors people over things. It seems important to build up the person who is to perform, before attempting to build the puppet, so that the source of the performance (the puppeteer) is identified and valued right from the start. This reverses the usual order of things, with the hope of strengthening the art of performing with puppets.

Chapter IV

THE PUPPETS

A puppet can be any object that is animated by human control.

The three requirements for a puppet are:

1) A form to be animated.
2) A person to do the animating.
3) A method of control that uses all or part of the puppeteer's body, or an extension of it through rods, strings, wires, magnets, or a combination of these.

A puppet may be as simple as a cardboard cutout on a stick, or as complex as a fully jointed marionette controlled by strings. The effectiveness of either one depends upon the imagination of the person supplying the voice and animation. An abstract shape, moved in a meaningful way, can be just as alive as shapes that suggest human or animal forms.

The puppeteer imparts these "life signs" to the object:

Breathing	Feeling
Moving	Thinking
Sensing	Speaking

Imagine a thin, wooden spoon as a haughty, bald soprano. What sound would she make? How would she move? Turn an eggbeater upside down and visualize it as a gangster type. Can he have shifty eyes? Does he sound menacing?

Objects that have never lived or moved before can take on life in the hands of a skillful puppeteer. Trees and flowers could go for a hike through the woods. The vegetables could do ballet. The walls, windows, tables, and chairs in a puppet cottage could march into place at the beginning of a scene and march off when it was over. In a puppet show, let the scenery shift for itself!

Some animated figures are puppetlike, without being true puppets. The automaton is a figure operated by machinery, usually in a limited and repeated cycle of movement. "Audioanimatronics" is the word coined for the moving figures at Disneyland. Pneumatic and hydraulic valves inside the figures produce movement when activated by sound impulses on a 32-channel tape. Amazing technology, but hardly puppetry. Real puppets must always have a human connection to sustain them. Anything else is a *robotnik*—a Czech word meaning "serf."

In 1930 James Juvenal Hayes developed "A Classification of Puppets," which Paul McPharlin adapted for his *Puppetry* yearbooks. All puppets were divided into two classes, round or flat, and each type was designated by numbers I through VII. The mode of operation noted both the position of the operator and the method of control. Variations were noted by lower case subheads.

I a. Marionette operated from above by string.
VII (1) b. Shadow Puppet (Opaque) operated from below by rod and string.

It is significant that this code for describing puppets included the location of the puppeteer. The variety of relationships is apparent in this list:

Side by Side
Ventriloquist
Variety Performer

Inside—Looking Out
  Mummenschanz's Soft Sculptures
  Big Bird, *Sesame Street*
Behind—Back-Up View
  Hand Puppets
  Shadow Puppets
  Bunraku (doll theatre)
Underneath—Looking Up
  Hand Puppets
  Rod Puppets
  Shadow Puppets

Above—Looking Down
  Marionettes (string puppets)
  Rod Puppets (Sicilian style)
  Finger Puppets

There may be psychological reasons for choosing a particular type of puppet, but it is not our purpose here to probe. Let those who enjoy lording it over the string puppets do so, along with those who would stand behind, or look up to their puppets. Along with the decision to be hidden or exposed, each individual should select the puppet disguise that gives the greatest satisfaction. These are some of the options.

Finger Puppet

The index and middle fingers are used as "legs" while the remaining fingers are tucked back out of sight. Finger-tips are wedged into the puppet's shoes. An elastic band encircling the wrist holds the puppet body upright. One puppeteer can manipulate two finger puppets simultaneously.

Hand Puppet (Also Known as a Glove or Fist Puppet)

The hand puppet consists of a head, neck, and hands attached to an empty costume. The hand, fingers, and forearm provide the skeleton inside; the wrist becomes the waist, and the forearm functions for the "legs." A variety of fingering positions are illustrated. The *Catalan puppet* is a variation, requiring three fingers

COURTESY MOLLIE FALKENSTEIN

Mollie Falkenstein demonstrates her original dancing figure puppet called the "Ballerette." The arms are controlled by strings.

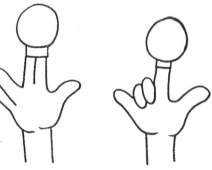

Three hand puppet positions.

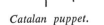

Catalan puppet.

to support the head and shoulder section. Puppet hands are at the end of tubes that fit on the puppeteer's fingers. Handling props with these extensions is something like using chopsticks to pick up rice. It takes practice. The Catalan puppet is proportioned to look like a much larger figure than the usual hand puppet. One puppeteer can manipulate two hand puppets simultaneously.

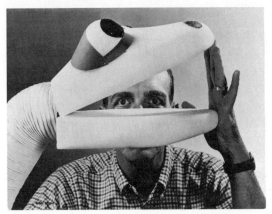

Mouth puppet and George Latshaw.

Mouth Puppet

This variation on the hand puppet is a traditional form for the Crocodile in Punch and Judy. The thumb is placed in the lower jaw; the remaining fingers slip into the top of the head.

Variations: Human mouth puppets can have dangling arms attached to the body, or the arms can be manipulated by rods from below. One puppeteer can handle two mouth puppets if the arms do not have to be controlled.

Humanette

This half-human, half-puppet combination capitalizes on a bizarre distortion of proportions between the life-sized head and hands growing out of the tiny body. The puppeteer's head and hands are thrust through slits in a black backdrop. The puppet body is attached to the puppeteer at the neck and wrists. The legs can be animated by running a string from the knee up to the puppeteer's hand.

Humanette.

Mask and Costume Puppet

A large-scale puppet can be an inside job. Illustrated is the villainous Jack-in-the-Box from a symphony production of Debussy's "La Boite à Joujoux" ("The Toy Box"). The puppet mask is supported atop the animator's head. The body is a circular tube of fabric held in shape by a series of hula hoops. The Jack-in-the-Box expands and contracts as the puppeteer stands or squats inside the framework. The false arm and hand rod allows the arms to extend or contract inside the sleeves. The ominous effect was intensified by building this puppet three times larger than the rest of the cast.

Jack-in-the-Box, mask and costume puppet from The Toy Box *by Claude Debussy.*

PHOTO:JIM SHEEHAN

Betty Polus of the Folk Puppet Theatre handles two shadow puppets backstage.

Shadow Puppet

The shadow puppet is a flat, jointed figure that is held against the back of a translucent screen. When the screen is lit from behind, the puppet casts a shadow on the screen for the audience on the other side. Asian shadows are constructed of stretched animal hide, which is perforated to produce intricate designs. Oriental translucent skin shadows are stained or dyed to produce colored shadows on the screen. A shadow puppet is controlled by one or two rods that extend either below or behind the figure. An expert can manipulate two shadow puppets simultaneously.

Rod Puppet

A central rod anchored in the head and neck creates the basic support and spine for the figure, which is operated from below. Slender rods extending down from the hands control arm positions. Walking is usually simulated through broad body movement, but sometimes legs are activated by strings attached where the thighs pivot at the hip. One pup-

PHOTO: RUSS HADDAD

Dr. Frank Ballard with the rod puppet Moor from Petrouchka, *produced at the University of Connecticut.*

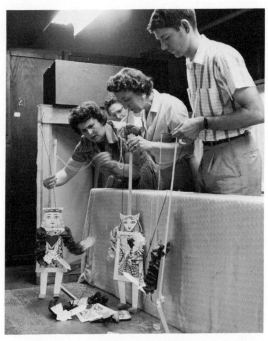

Summer session students in Theatre Arts at The Pennsylvania State University manipulate paper, cloth, and cardboard rod puppets, Sicilian style.

peteer uses both hands to control a rod puppet of this construction.

Rod Puppet—Sicilian

These handsome wooden figures of knights in armor are controlled from above by an iron rod attached to the head. The right hand (sword hand) is controlled by another iron rod. The left hand (shield hand) is controlled by a cord. To set the legs in motion, the figure is jounced up and down until the feet swing back and forth. It can be dropped into a noble stance, or moved in great strides across the stage. Armored puppets stand 3 to 4 feet high and may weigh 50 to 75 pounds. Nonspeaking puppets may be suspended from hooks while they "listen." In performance, an acting, dashing rod puppet is a one-person-one-puppet workout.

String Puppet—Marionette

A marionette can be constructed of wood, cloth, plastic wood, papier mâché, Celastic, or any combination of materials. A basic marionette is a jointed figure controlled by nine strings running from the head, shoulders, seat, hands, and knees to a wooden controller above. The controller may be upright or horizontal. Head action occurs by adjusting the angle of the controller; walking and gesturing are done by pulling specific strings. Marionettes may be suspended from hooks above the stage, allowing one manipulator to bring additional characters into the scene if the action is simple.

Or None of the Above

The puppets I have described can all be handled by one person. Sometimes the scale or intricacy of a puppet concept may require the use of more than one animator. Teams of two or more can produce these special effects.

Pierrot at the Circus, *Mrs. Vatite and Wayne. Designed by Arlyn Coat, Coad Canada Puppets.*

Bunraku-za Theatre, Japanese Doll Theater, Osaka.

Dancing Horse—(Vaudeville or circus act)

Two-person team. One animates the front end of the horse costume; the other brings up the rear.

Bunraku—Japanese Doll Theatre

Three-man teams. Each member is responsible for moving a portion of the total figure. Manipulators are dressed in black to minimize their visibility in back of the doll.

Chinese Dragon (Festival)

One person animates the dragon head from inside while numerous assistants stand under the attached body covering to support the spine, provide the legs, and move the monster in an undulating, snakelike fashion.

Puppets come in all sizes, shapes, weights, and methods of control. The puppeteers' disguise allows them to be in it, to be out of it, or even to be above it all.

Chapter V

DESIGN

Design is the magnet that attracts artists and crafts persons from outside the theatre to try their hand at puppetry. They see the puppet as a means of channeling the skills they have into a form that has life, movement, and sound. Paul Klee, the painter; Tony Sarg, the illustrator; and W. A. Dwiggins, the type and book designer, experimented with puppets. Even the fascinating wire sculpture figures of Alexander Calder's Circus have elements of designed movement that we associate with puppetry.

The person who lacks design training may feel self-conscious about putting an idea down on paper for fear of making a mistake. What comes out at the end of the pencil never seems to match the vision going on in the mind. The problem of designing with a pencil is the eraser, for it hovers over the work ready to "correct" any mistakes even before they occur. It can be very inhibiting, so we shall dismiss the pencil sketch approach to puppet design and suggest two alternate methods that are quick and fun and hold better promise of success.

DIRECT ENCOUNTER WITH MATERIALS

Fern Zwickey, Professor Emeritus of the Art Education Department of Wayne State University, is a master at inspiring beginners to turn out puppets in a single session. She may show a sample or two or three to start people thinking about what puppets might look like and how they are put together, but then she turns the group loose on the boxes and boxes of "puppet stuff" she has brought along. What happens is a combination of Christmas, bargain basement, and rummage sale as people dig and delve through the wondrous assortment of materials she has provided. Styrofoam balls, wooden spoons, plastic scoops (That looks like a head, maybe), feathers, fur, felt, fringe (That's the kind of hair I want on mine), buttons, beads, metal discs and wooden shapes (How do these look for the eyes?), yarn, string, and sticky tape (Where did you find the fabric scraps?), colored paper, pins and glue, pipe cleaners, springs and wire, and all the things that are needed to put it together. (Have you finished already? I'm starting on my second one.)

At the end of the session there is an amazing array of delightful puppets. There is decided variety, because each person has encountered the materials, made selections, and assembled a puppet that is different from every other puppet there. Mrs. Zwickey sparks the creativity in the group. Once a person has made a puppet by the assemblage or collage method, s/he will be on the lookout for interesting materials to make more.

A CUT-PAPER APPROACH

You will need construction paper in assorted colors, scissors, and, later on, some paste, glue, or rubber cement for sticking down the paper.

Our first project will be to design a puppet head. You will be limited to using simple, basic shapes. Discussion is easier if all participants use the same elements.

Basic Shapes

These include a square, a rectangle, an oval, a diamond, a pear-shape, a heart, a triangle, a circle, a hexagon, a trapezoid, and an ellipse.

Pick one of the shapes for a puppet head (a) because the shape suits a puppet character you have in mind; or (b) to see what character could grow out of the shape you select.

Take a sheet of the colored construction paper, fold it in half, and estimate that the finished head will be 6 inches from top to bottom. Use no pencils, markers, or ruler. Make a bold guess and cut freehand. When you open the cut paper, both sides will match, and the fold will mark center. Lay the shape flat and study the surface. Imagine eyes, nose, mouth, ears, cheeks, eyebrows, and hair.

From other colors of paper cut basic shapes for features. Use any of the shapes listed above, or add half circles, crescents, stars, almond shapes, etc.

Place (do not glue) the cut-paper features on the head shape to develop a face. Reposition the features as often as you wish to check the effects. Save all scraps from cutting, because you may find interesting shapes in the negative forms that you might not have thought of cutting out directly. Study your first design. Does it look like a puppet? What character do you see? Look at the other designs in the group. Could you guess what characters they had created?

Using a variety of different shapes helps the audience to identify each separate character at a distance. Basic shapes also encourage us to move away from an imitation of reality toward bold masks and strong caricatures to carry our message. It is difficult to get caught up in a lot of fussy detail when the colors and forms are so simple.

With this open-ended approach, the design stays fluid until you are ready to set it. It is no problem to rearrange, substitute, or alter the features until they achieve the effect you want. I call this a "push-face" assembly, because the features are pushed around on the basic head shape until a winning combination clicks into place.

To continue our experiment, we can change the placement of the features to see what happens to the proportions of the face. The mid-placement of the features on the first head is closest to human proportion and is rather plain. The second cartoon uses a high placement of the features—it also has two mouths. Cover the lower mouth with your fingertip and see how the proportion of the jaw increases. Place your finger under the nose and note how the lowered mouth suggests sagging jowls. A low placement of all the features changes the proportion of the forehead. By placing features to one side of the center, the face seems to have turned in that direction.

In another experiment, exaggerate a single feature for emphasis. Use the head design you have made. Decide on the single most important feature. Cut it out in a larger size, and place it over the one that is already in place. What happens to the effect? Enlarge the feature once again. Reduce the size of the remaining features with new cutouts. Hair, moustaches, beards, and glasses are elements that could be exaggerated.

An emotional facial expression can be heightened by the use of color. Animated cartoons frequently use this technique to underline the mood of the character. From the list below, select a color and cut out a shape that matches the mood for:

Four cartoon faces.

Three line drawings with exaggerated features.

feeling "blue"
red as a beet
white as a sheet
brown as a berry
green with envy
in the pink
turning purple

What would be the appropriate emotional expression for each color? Study the expressions of your own face in a mirror if you need help placing the features to express mood.

As a final experiment, select a character, cut a shape, and build features for it. See how much you can take away and still retain the *essence* of that character in a recognizable form. The secret of good design is in knowing what to leave out, as well as what to put in. Many effective puppet heads have been made with no surface decoration on the face at all. Changes of expression seem to take place as the blank face catches light and shadow under lights. The lack of detail allows the audience imagination to fill in.

When you have finished the face design for this project, glue down the features on the head. Glue the head design to a sheet of black construction paper. Place your design at one side of the room and move to the opposite side to observe it. Does the design carry at that distance? Is there enough contrast between colors? Would outlining help to sharpen any of the features? Would it be a good makeup for your ultimate disguise?

After these experiments we should feel that design time is idea-generating time. It should be a means of pretesting and refining ideas. The final design is a plan for the construction of the puppet in three dimensions, using line, form, color, texture, and materials.

DESIGN INPUT FROM THE SCRIPT

Costume and scene designers in the theatre work from a known quantity—the script. They read it carefully to discover in the written lines and descriptive passages all the information they need to understand the characters and locales. When they have a thorough knowledge of the script, they consult with the director on the interpretation. The design process does not begin until they have identified, analyzed, and generalized about the visual elements of production.

Pushbutton Planet, a puppet production for the Pacific Conservatory of the Performing Arts, posed some interesting design problems. The theme dealt with the isolation of persons in a future world of advanced technology. The inhabitants had no names; they were identified by computer numbers. They had no contact with each other, for each had his/her own private space capsule, and all needs and wants were supplied by the remarkable push-button system inside. Communication took place between television images.

To interpret the image of "isolation," each puppet was placed inside the circle of a hula hoop. This served to frame the separation of each figure as the bubbles floated and drifted

Pushbutton Planet, *Puppet (041–140) in space cap-sule. Manipulator: George Latshaw.*

Duchess and Baby from Alice in Wonderland *by the Bil Baird Marionettes.*

Pushbutton Planet, *Woman. Designer: George Lat-shaw.*

52

through space. The environment had affected the physical shape of the inhabitants. The parts of the body that were still used remained large; those that were not were minimized. The heads were quite large, and the arms were very long as they reached for the pushbuttons. The bodies were small, and the legs were almost nonexistent. Hair had almost disappeared in this society, but note the designs tattooed on the head of the lady. In contrast to the Pushbutton people was the Blue Garoo, who contemplated on a mountaintop far away. He had a body of more normal proportions and eyeballs that could float out of his head. Design helped to underscore the playwright's point.

Bil Baird is to puppetry what Walt Disney is to film animation, an artist with an unmistakable style. His puppets are designed with such verve that they seem to leap off the printed page or puppet stage with equal ease. The Baird production of *Alice in Wonderland* remained true to the Tenniel illustrations for the book without losing that special zest that made it Bil Baird's cast of hand, rod, and string puppets playing the familiar roles. Alice appeared in two sizes, a live actress and a marionette sharing the part in different scenes. Note the Duchess and the strength of feeling that comes from the simple form of the baby on her lap.

Basil Milovsoroff's innovative design work has been inspiring to many puppeteers. Early in his career, he carved charming peasant types for his Russian folk tale plays. Then he experimented with root sculptures and simple forms, evolving into a contemporary rod puppet of great power. His three savages for *Sinbad* have vivid raffia costumes that rustle and swirl. The figure on the right creates its own sound effects. The bright orange beak claps together when the figure stomps up and down. The ball hanging at the side of the head hits the hollowed head form with a thonk-thonk as the figure is twisted side to side. It is primitive perfection. The Center for the Arts at Muhlenberg College honored the artist with a two-month exhibition, "Basil Milovsoroff: WORLDS, Sculpture Styles in the Puppet Theatre," which opened Dec. 5, 1976.

Milovsoroff's sound and motion experiments remind us that the puppet designer is not concerned with appearances alone, but goes right to the core of what is under the costume and makeup to the anatomy of the figure itself, and even to the materials from which it is made. The puppet does not have to be a copy of the human actor's skeletal structure and jointing system; it can be constructed to any design with any materials that achieve the effect. Eugene and Galina Naum's *Music Hall Show* dancer is the picture of lightness and grace twirling across the stage. Unhampered by any human anatomy, the movement flows through the puppet's yarn construction to suggest graceful limbs. Motion materials that the designer uses include springs, feathers, roping, yarn, fringe, plastic tubing, metal chains, and wooden beads. When Goodyear Tire and Rubber Company thought of bringing two of its industrial products to life, they thought of puppets. Designed by Paul Berger and constructed by me, the two characters Beltram and Hosea discuss the strong points of conveyer belts and industrial hoses in a short film at the Goodyear World of Rubber.

Body-painting has long been the vogue in the puppet world—to simulate the tights and opera hose that, if used, would restrict the movements of a jointed marionette. Eric Bramall's Two Harlequins, of the Harlequin Puppet Theatre, Rhos-on-Sea, Colwyn Bay, North Wales, are properly attired in their painted diamonds. In puppetry, the body can be the costume or the costume can be the body, for there is no human actor to clothe and the designer is in charge of all creation.

The three Cannibals from The 8th Voyage of Sinbad; *sound and motion rod puppets by Basil Milovsoroff (1952).*

The yarn construction Dancer, created by Eugene and Galina Naum for A Music Hall Show.

Beltram and Hosea, designed by Paul Berger and constructed by George Latshaw.

Eric Bramall and The Two Harlequins (with painted tights).

Chapter VI

IMAGES IN ACTION

There is no guard patrolling the borders of puppetry, checking passports to admit performers and exclude others. It is a "foreign" country, nonetheless, and it would be wise to learn the language if one intends to stay. We all know how to speak "people," and how to move in "people" ways, but it takes some translating to speak "puppet" and to move in "puppet" ways. The puppet, also, must learn our movement vocabulary to speak back to us in actions that we can understand. This, then, will be a blitz course in how to translate universal body language from "people" to "puppet" and back again.

For the first lesson we need a simple rehearsal puppet. None of this nonsense of having the puppets arrive in full costume and makeup to charm their way out of a disciplined work session. Actors, dancers, and musicians practice and rehearse in casual attire. A puppet in training should follow their example by working diligently before acquiring the trappings of performance.

The hand puppet is the ideal figure for a start, because so much of it is ready-made. The puppeteer's hand, fingers, and forearm are not only the basis for the puppet body and limbs, but also the means of control. The only thing to be built is a hand-puppet head. (See Chapter IX for directions to make a styrofoam head with finger stall for the neck.) An unpainted bead or button is allowed for the nose (to make it easier to tell the front from the back of the head.) "Rehearsal puppets" should have no other features, no color, and no costumes. Several neutral puppets of this sort working together will have to distinguish themselves by movement alone, and not by surface decoration. A white cotton work glove may be used to cover the puppeteer's hand, but this is not essential.

BASIC TERMS, TRANSLATING HUMAN HAND TO PUPPET BODY

In the diagram below, the parts of the human hand and arm have been relabeled to describe their functions in a puppet body. Though it may seem ridiculous to find the ribs located below the elbow and the brain extending from the neck, it is essential to "translate" the familiar moving parts into other terms before we can expect new patterns of movement.

Instinctively, we use our hands and fingers in certain ways regardless of the covering, be it gloves, mittens, bandages, or hand puppets. Watch young children with hand puppets, and note the speed with which the puppet action moves to pushing, hitting, and pinching. The hands inside these puppets are still acting as hands, doing the things that children do with their hands—push, hit, and pinch. The puppet is simply another covering, a glorified boxing glove, until adults put a stop to it.

Adult beginners do not resort to violence, but their puppets often seem to be afflicted with a bad case of the jitters. Index fingers waggling and shaking and/or middle finger and thumb constantly tapping together cause the puppet to do a great deal of meaningless head-bobbing and hand-clapping to accent every spoken word, because the hand inside is speaking "people" instead of "puppet." Human actors would be fired on the spot for waggling

55

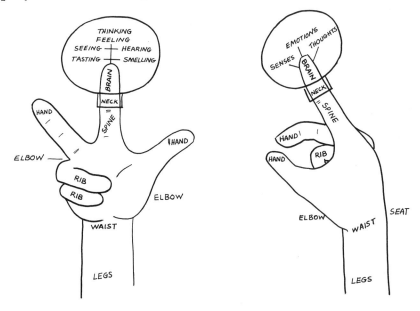

PHOTO: MAX TORO

Front and side view line drawing of a human hand relabeled to describe its new functions in a puppet body.

"Community members" in a show for a cooperative organization, Títeres de Borinquen, Rafael Ruiz, and Francisco Torres, Puerto Rico.

their heads and clapping their hands through every speech, and puppets who have that habit should also be kept off the stage. Control the urge to make the puppet act like a dodo; give it the dignity of specific gestures; study the diagram until the native language of the hand is replaced by puppet action.

A puppet "at ease" will hold both hands together in front of the body. Strong, visible gestures will open out from this position (pointing, waving, reacting with surprise, etc.). If the puppet's hands are always spread wide, there is no place to go except inward, which is a less compelling move. Nor should the puppet's hands be up in the air (again, fingers relating to each other in a comfortable position, rather than "puppet hands") unless it has been commanded to "Reach for the sky, pardner!"

With these preliminary cautions out of the way, it is time to translate "people" body language into "puppet" movement. This is easier to understand by taking one body area at a time, and by having the human demonstrate the action and explain the meaning so that the puppet can repeat the action and the meaning.

LESSON ONE—BODY MECHANICS

Movement for the Head	Meaning
Nod front to back	yes
Turn side to side *	no
Cocked to one side	listening, thinking
Dropped forward	tired, or sad
Rotating, round-and-round	dizzy, faint, bedazzled
————	————

Continue the list of head movements and meanings. Do some movements have more than one meaning?

———

* The hand puppet cannot turn the head independently side to side without also moving the body. In such a case, the puppet must simulate (by adding body movement) or substitute for the action—nodding from side to side—until it can use hands placed on the cheeks to gently turn the head from side to side.

Movement for Hands	Meaning
Clap together	applause, approval, hurry
Wave one hand, fast or slow	"Goodbye!", "Hi!"
Point right hand and back	"over there"
Point left hand and back	that, those, them
Both hands open out	surprise, all, everything
Rub hands together	greed, glee, enthusiasm
One hand beckons	"Come here"
One hand to head	pensive, thoughtful
Hand scratches head	puzzled, thinking
Hands on cheeks, turn head	no, unbelievable
Hands rotate around each other	exercise
Hands, arms crisscross, recross	embarrassment, nervousness
Head drops, both hands touch behind neck	chagrin
Elbow in hand, chin in other hand	pondering
————	————
————	————

Add to the list. Try to stump the puppet with an action; then find a solution. A favorite is asking the puppet to snap its fingers. The puppet can simulate the action of the hand, and if the sound is made at the same time, it creates the illusion that the puppet snapped its fingers to prove it was as versatile as the human.

Movement for Waist and Torso	Meaning
Bow forward	welcome, searching on ground
Bend backward	looking up, surprise
Rotate round and round	wind up to strike or faint
Thrust hip to one side	a hip bump

Bend to right side, bend to left side	morning exercise
Bend forward, butt with head	move on, tackle
Bend over, touch toes	use top of head, because hands won't reach!
Shake torso	a shimmy
_____	_____
_____	_____

Movement for Legs

Translating the movement of two legs into the action of the single pedestal provided by the puppeteer's forearm may seem impossible to the novice, but it is another of the theatrical illusions that hand puppets can create. A slight turn of the puppet body to the right and then to the left as it moves forward will simulate the right step, left step of walking on two legs. Variations on this basic walk will develop unique character walks.

Slow, hesitant steps	Is the puppet shy, timid, aged, or blind?
Short, bouncy steps	Is the puppet youthful, perky, athletic, silly?
Swooping steps with nose in the air	Is the puppet haughty, regal, or absent-minded?
Body hunched forward, steps heavily accented on one side	Is the puppet an old crone, a lame beggar, a peg-legged pirate?

Think of other ways of moving and walking, and make a list of descriptive action verbs. Simulate these movements with the puppet—and add sound effects, using your own feet, when it will help to clarify the action (i.e., marching, tap-dancing, stomping, galloping, etc.).

Bounce	Jump	Skate
Cavort	Kick	Skip
Crawl	Leap	Slide
Dawdle	Limp	Slither

Dive	Lope	Soar
Fall	March	Stagger
Flounce	Run	Stomp
Gallop	Scramble	Swim
Glide	Shuffle	Tiptoe
Hop		

Were you able to get your puppet off the ground for a hop and a jump? Did you simulate the preparation: the bending down; the one-two-three readiness; the spring in the air; the landing with sharp force; and the bounce back after hitting the ground? Watch a person jump and land. Work on the "spring" coming from inside the puppet. Show the landing and "give" as if meeting solid ground.

Can the puppet hop from right foot to left foot and back? If the puppet body rises in an arc and tilts toward the landing side each time, it will give the impression it has shifted from one foot to the other. Widen the arc and slow down the movement to turn the hop into a graceful ballet leap.

Try to simulate "sitting" on the edge of a table. The back of the wrist represents the seat of the pants. If the puppet "sits" with back to audience, we do not see what happens to the legs as the body is lowered, and we assume "knees" bend into the proper position. Try kneeling, without knees. What happens to the body line to suggest this position? Could the puppet curtsey? Can it waver, faint, and do a fall? Continue to experiment until you have built a repertoire of "walks" and leg movements for the puppet.

Lesson Two—Sensory Exercises

If a puppet does not know what to do with itself on stage, it may fall into the trap of doing nothing or doing too much that is meaningless. The same sensory awareness exercises that actors use can provide the puppet with actions that are rich, inventive, and remarkable to behold.

Sight. Since there are no eyes on the rehearsal puppet, the puppeteer must learn to "act" the sight by pointing the puppet's nose (and eyes) in the direction of the object it wishes to see. Most puppets' eyes are painted on in fixed position, so it is important to practice focusing directly. Ask a person to use an index finger as a pointer to trace random patterns in the air. Let your puppet follow the moving point with its eyes. The partner acting as pointer should trace varied patterns: fast, slow, high, low, circle, square, triangle, figure eight, etc. When the puppet can track the moving point without being tricked, it is beginning to "see" for itself. As a reward, two colored paper circles can be pinned to the styrofoam puppet head to serve as the eyes in succeeding exercises.

Hearing. Puppets "listen" by focusing their eyes on the speaker, just as actors do. If the puppet's eyes are not on the speaker, then its mind is somewhere else, and it should be reprimanded for trying to steal stage. Eye contact—actor to actor, or puppet to puppet—indicates attention.

Exercise for 3 or 4 Puppets

Have each puppet introduce itself to the others. Run through the group from left to right. Listeners must turn to focus their eyes on each speaker. Repeat the exercise to vary the order in which introductions are made. Do the listening puppets direct our attention to each speaker by giving eye focus each time?

Exercise for Individual Puppet

Have the puppet "hear" and respond to the following sounds:

Whispered gossip	Rock-and-roll band
Frankenstein foot- steps	Dragon's roar
Ringing telephone	Drag-strip racer
Buzzing bee	Lullaby
Clock striking mid- night	Ambulance siren

How long does it take the puppet to "hear," recognize the sound, and react? Could you tell each time where the sound originated?

Touch. The puppet can expand its movement capability by being sensitive to textures.

Have the puppet touch or stroke imaginary objects with the qualities listed below. Can the observers tell what the object was from the puppet's pantomime of touching and reacting?

Smooth	Heavy	Cold
Sharp	Hot	Cuddly
Rough	Tickly	

Exercise for Individual Puppet

Use a small prop pillow. Have the puppet prepare it for the most comfortable headrest in the world by plumping it, placing it, testing it, rearranging it, and finally using it to settle down for a snooze.

Taste. The puppet can pantomime a taste test of the items listed below, and share its approval or disapproval of each.

Sweet honey	Slippery spaghetti
Sour pickles	Hard rolls
Hot soup	Chewy caramels
Cold cuts	Bitter medicine

Sound effects, accompanying the puppet action, will heighten the illusion that the puppet is using its mouth to savor or spit out what it has tasted.

Smell. Have the puppet react to the following odors:

Exotic perfume	Burning trash
Rotten eggs	Baking bread
_____	_____
_____	_____

Add to the list. Is the reaction to smell centered on the nose alone, or do other parts of the body react as well? Since the sense of smell comes through the nose, it leads us to the breathing mechanism of the puppet.

THE BREATH OF LIFE AND ALL THOSE SOUNDS

Try making these sounds for the puppet, remembering that movement and sound together create the total illusion.

Inhale-Exhale	Wheeze	Hiccup
Cough	Snicker	Giggle

Sneeze	Snort	Gulp
Sigh	Laugh	Pant
Snore	Cry	Yech
Yawn	Gasp	Harrumph
Sniff	Groan	

You will have noticed how much the entire body of the puppet enters into reacting to the sense exercises. It is not just the head (facial expression) but the entire figure at work that expresses the puppet's attitude toward the sense experience. Attitudes and feelings grow into emotions, which are the actors' tools of theatrical communication. When we can empathize with what the actor (or puppet) is feeling, we take another step toward "life" on the stage.

LESSON THREE—EMOTIONS AND FEELINGS

Using the movement language developed in previous lessons, devise a scene in which two or three puppets could pantomime the following emotions:

Love	Anger	Jealousy
Fear	Surprise	Greed
Joy	Grief	

LESSON FOUR—PLAYTIME

The more the hand puppet is tested, the more one discovers its capabilities. Playing games is another way of building skills by expanding experience. These should be done for no other purpose than to have fun. The games may be played by one puppeteer manipulating two puppets or by several puppeteers each handling one participating puppet.

Blindman's Buff	Elephant Walk
Pease Porridge Hot	Tag
Hopscotch	Hide-and-seek
Running Broad Jump	Tug-of-War
Catch—Bean Bag	Leapfrog
Pillow Fight	Follow the Leader

LESSON FIVE—HANDLING OBJECTS

The puppet adds to its credibility by man-aging and maneuvering stage properties scaled to the puppet or borrowed from the human world. Some actions that a single human can perform may require two puppets. Cutting a shape from a piece of paper requires two puppets; one to hold the paper steady, the other to snip out the shape with the scissors. Assemble the props required for the following exercises, substituting an empty bottle and pantomime for the shampoo, etc. Puppeteers can sit at a table, using the table surface as the flooring or playboard for props that remain in position.

Wash hair: Use a bucket, dunk head, apply shampoo, make suds, rinse, grope for towel, fluff dry, style hair.

Read a book: Open cover, turn pages, scan lines, react to text.

Mix a cake: Use a real bowl, spoon, measuring cups; pantomime flour, cracking eggs, adding milk, etc.

Scrub the floor: Tote bucket, find spots, really scrub with brush or rag, rinse in pail, wring dry.

Use a fly swatter: Spot the fly, track it, sneak up on it, get it!

Balloon on a string: Play with balloon, bat it, bounce it, balance it, chase it, toss and catch it, pop it.

Soap bubbles: Dip bubble wand in liquid, wave wand to make bubbles, watch them drift, float, and disappear.

Use a feather or fan: Cool, tickle, cover, and entice another puppet.

Costume pieces are also props that puppets can manipulate effectively. Tassels and fringe provide additional movement, as do capes, hats, earrings, feathers, silk kerchiefs, shawls, watch chains, aprons, beads, and long ties. These costume accessories extend the range of movement. Select one to add to your rehearsal puppet to see what use can be made of it.

LESSON SIX—SHALL WE DANCE?

Some knowledge of the basic steps and movement patterns is necessary to capture the essence of the dances listed below. Our resource is human movement; our object is to add versatility to the puppet movement. It is suggested that the puppets be held overhead so that when the puppeteer below turns completely around, the puppet also has made a complete turn. In the square dance, one puppeteer can be used for each participating puppet. In the waltz, one puppeteer might hold

both puppets aloft to coordinate the graceful turns.

Square dance	Ballet pas de deux
Waltz	Conga line
Tap dance	Rumba or Tango
The Bump	Boogie

To learn about images in action, we have

PHOTO: PATRICK LECOQ

MUMMENSCHANZ, Swiss Mask-Mine Troupe, discovering new ways to use the human form.

PHOTO: PATRICK LECOQ

MUMMENSCHANZ, a giant animated soft sculpture.

COURTESY BASIL MILOVSOROFF

"Insectalia" (experimental) by Basil Milovsoroff.

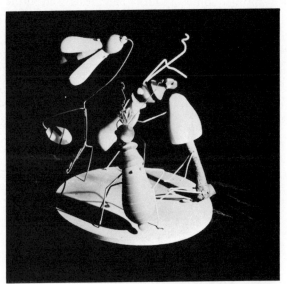

COURTESY BASIL MILOVSOROFF

"Insectalia" in silhouette by Basil Milovsoroff.

observed the human world's movement in order to translate it into puppet action. The same process can be used to discover the potential for string puppets, rod puppets, and shadows. Each type of figure has its strengths and shortcomings—and it is wise to test each puppet for its movement potential before trying to express yourself through it in a production.

Some puppet artists would object to this whole system of training based on body language of humans, declaring that it results in puppets as poor imitations of human actors rather than free creative beings apart. They envision the puppet in more abstract terms, an animated sculpture that determines its own choreography. Their view is valid, for the puppet, after all, is only an image, which can be designed with any degree of realism or abstraction the creator wishes. The success of abstract puppetry also depends on the images' ability to communicate with the audience. For us to fully understand, appreciate, and *care* about the image, it must speak to us in a movement language we can identify and understand.

An outstanding example of communication through abstract objects was performed (not by puppeteers) by the Swiss Mask-Mime Troupe named Mummenschanz. Half of their exciting program was devoted to animating abstract soft sculptures. The forms were droll shapes that did not at all resemble the humans inside. A blob resembling a plump pillow inched onstage and, in exploring the space around it, discovered the top of the platform against which it was resting. Portions of the blob reached out for a grip or hold, but could not manage to hang on long enough for the bottom portion to rise to that level. After approaching the problem in various ways, the blob finally got all of itself to the top. It was a triumph. A living form had met and mastered an immovable object. Because there were no human forms or voices, the audience could perceive the very essence of what it means to yearn, struggle, and achieve. It was the art of puppetry presented by a brilliant mime troupe.

The Alwin Nikolais Dance Company is another group that has made masterful use of the principles of puppetry. In one popular work, the dancers were encased in tubular forms of stretch fabric. The changing body positions inside manipulated the material to form oblongs, triangles, diamonds, and cones. Changing light projections on these movable forms enhanced the impression that one had stumbled into a totally new world of form and feeling. Choreographer Nikolais has shown us a new potential for puppetry through dance.

Could a Square bounce up and down before sliding across the stage to bump into a gently rocking Circle? Could the Square not bow and apologize for knocking the Circle for a loop, and could the Square not seek some soft wall where it could rub its bruised side? Could the Circle not observe with disdain? Could the Square then tiptoe over on one point and jump "BOO" at the Circle? Could the Circle shake with anger, split in two, with the half circles chomping down on the trembling Square to devour it all? Pick your image; pick your message; but communicate.

Chapter VII

VOICES AND SOUND EFFECTS

Mirrors and other reflecting surfaces may do us more charm than good. They focus all our attention on appearances and force us to see ourselves as others see us. If we do not care for the image, we can attempt to change the face, the hair, the physique, and the clothes into something more pleasing. While we struggle with diet, exercise, grooming, and wardrobe, the voice inside the body remains the same.

Today we can hear ourselves as others hear us through the magic of the home tape recorder. Many people, hearing their own voices for the first time, react with shock and dismay. They tend to think the equipment is at fault for distorting "their" voice to sound like a stranger's. It is curious that what we hear "inside," when we speak, is not the same sound that another person hears on the "outside." Nor are we aware of how much our voices reveal about us—our age, sex, physical condition, emotional state, and regional upbringing. Aspiring puppeteers would do well to use the tape recorder to get acquainted with the sound of their own voices, for those voices will provide at least 50 percent of the illusion in a puppet show.

The second step is to direct the reader to the books *Acting* and *The Actor's Voice* in this *Theatre Student* series (see Bibliography). Follow the practical suggestions in the section on Voice Production. Puppeteers should develop strong, clear voices that will project through the masking and draperies of the puppet stage. Though it is possible to use amplified sound, puppet voices sound more natural and more appropriate to the puppet scale if they are done live. The unassisted voice

reminds the puppeteer to make a continuing, conscious effort to reach the audience vocally.

A third step in the search for puppet voices involves listening. Many of us accept sound in a very passive way. It is there, and it is what it is. We identify sound, but we do not analyze it to discover the general principles by which it was made. The puppeteer must become an astute listener to build a repertoire of interesting character voices.

Certain figures in the entertainment world have such distinctive voices that they could be identified immediately from their speech. Mimics and impressionists capitalize on their ability to reproduce such famous voices. These are a few of the performers whose voices are easy to recognize:

Rex Harrison	W. C. Fields
Carol Channing	Mae West
Marilyn Monroe	Howard Cosell
Humphrey Bogart	Peter Lorre

In another category are the voices of famous cartoon characters. Because the cartoon images are not realistic, their voices can be more stylized. There is a hint of caricature in the manner of speaking for each character. Mel Blanc originated many of the major voices for *Looney Tunes,* and Jim Backus provided the droll voice for the nearsighted *Mr. Magoo.*

Bugs Bunny	Donald Duck
Porky Pig	Mickey Mouse
Woody Woodpecker	Mr. Magoo

Do not overlook the world around you as a rich resource for character voices. Listen to your family, your neighbors, your friends. Listen to strangers in grocery stores, restaurants, elevators, and theatre lobbies. Which voices are the most striking? What does the voice tell you about the person? Which elements are most characteristic in the voices you hear? Use the list below to assist in your descriptions.

Pitch—Normal: voice placed in a comfortable middle range.

Low: several notes below normal down to basso profundo.

High: several notes above the normal range.

Falsetto: an artificially high-pitched voice in the musical "soprano" range for a man or woman.

Speed—Fast: the mile-a-minute talker.

Slow: the leisurely drawl.

Normal: a direct, even rate of speaking.

Erratic: stop-and-go with variable speeds.

Rhythmic: a patterned cadence to the phrasing.

Volume—Loud: big, booming, and hearty.

Soft: a strain to catch all the words, quiet, subdued.

Normal: easy to hear clearly.

Force, Stress—Does the speaker "punch" certain words to stress their importance—some of the time, or all of the time? Does the speaker have a bland way of speaking, because no stress is given?

Color—Does the voice help us to "see" what we are hearing? Do descriptive words come alive with meaning because of the vibrant way they are spoken? Try to say the following words in such a way that their meaning comes alive:

Chilly	Swift	Beautiful
Icy	Hard	Gorgeous
Slow	Gentle	Tingling

Can the voice "color" a word to reveal our attitude about it? Try these.

Spinach	Is it broken?

Income tax	Such a clown
So high and mighty	That's highway robbery!

Quality—The manner in which the vocal tone is produced affects the "character" of the voice.

Clear: Well-modulated standard stage speech.

Suave: soft, smooth, and velvety; or oily.

Hollow: Deep and resonant.

Dry: clipped, without resonance.

Gruff: gravelly, guttural.

Nasal: upper resonance, flat.

Shrill: high, harsh, pinched, rasping.

Cracked: the high-low break as in the voice change of some teenage speech.

A word of caution before attempting the changes in voice quality. Ease into it gradually, and do not push your voice to the point of strain. At any sign of discomfort, stop, relax, yawn, rotate the head to relax the neck muscles, and discontinue the vocal exercises. Any character voices that cause strain could damage the vocal cords. Recognize the limitations of your instrument, and stay within the range that is comfortable, relaxed, and without strain. A good puppet voice is one you can sustain through an hour's performance without fatigue or stress.

The following exercises can be done by one person working alone or by each member of a group. At this early stage of experimenting, I would suggest that no recording device be used. If you are alone, work to please yourself. If you are in a group, use the others as a "sounding board" after you have determined how it sounds inside and how it feels. You will discover that you can "think" your way into a different voice. Cultivate the character attitudes that will produce the voice you want. Take time to have fun with voices, and remember that you are working to please people, and not striving to get a perfect playback from the machine. Your own confidence is an important contributor to your progress.

Exercise #1—Age

Historic moments for the life of You! Trace your development through sample sounds and phrases from each period: The baby, the child, the adolescent, the teenager, the young adult, the mature adult, the golden ager.

Exercise #2—Sex

Puppeteers frequently do voices for both sexes in a solo show. Select three of the character roles listed below. Speak for each in a female voice, then speak for each in a male voice.

Truck driver	Olympic Medal winner
Brain surgeon	Beauty contestant
Corporation president	Explorer

Exercise #3—Physical Condition

Remember what it feels like to speak:

when you have a bad cold and runny nose.

when you have stuffed yourself at the smorgasbord.

when you are tired, drowsy, half asleep.

when you have run upstairs to get to the phone.

when you are in tip-top physical shape.

Exercise #4—Emotional States

Can you recall what happens to your voice when you are emotionally involved? Say several sentences to let the following feelings show through your voice.

Irritated	Excited	Nervous
Afraid	Cheerful	Flabbergasted
Secretive	Loving	Tender

Exercise #5—Regional Dialect

As a roving reporter, think of a question you might ask in a cross-country poll. In your own voice, ask the question as the reporter, then respond as a resident of each region listed below.

South	New England	Midwest
West	Brooklyn	Bronx
South of the border	Hawaii	Puerto Rico

Exercise #6—Ethnic Dialect

Dialects are easier to recognize than reproduce. It requires careful study to capture the spirit, flavor, and nuance of another language adapted to English. These suggestions are included for future reference.

British	Russian	Irish
French	German	Japanese
Spanish	Italian	African

Singing, whistling, humming, and clucking are extensions of the human voice that can add to character portrayals. The Bronx cheer, or raspberry, is another sound you might need. Avoid speech impediments; the lisp, stutter, and cleft-palate speech are handicaps and should not be used for comic characterization. Good taste is a requisite for good puppetry.

Animal characters are popular on the puppet stage, both in speaking parts and as barnyard pets and jungle beasts. The puppeteer should be prepared to take on the animal kingdom: geese, ducks, dogs, cats, lions, pigs, roosters, chickens, baby birds, crows, bluejays, whippoorwills, horses, and cows, plus the inevitable bees, mosquitoes, crickets, and frogs.

Other backstage sound effects that might be required include vocal renditions of turbines, motor bikes, steam engines, fog horns, locomotives, sirens, antique cars, telephone bells, bicycle pumps, buzzers, airplanes, helicopters, and reasonable facsimiles of wind, thunder, and many others.

In a production with several players, the sound dimensions might be extended through the use of a simple wind and percussion section. Entrances, character "themes," dramatic moments might be underscored in the manner of the Japanese Kabuki theatre by using wood blocks, triangles, bells, ratchets, slide whistles, maracas, drums, tambourines, toy xylophones, chimes, and cymbals. A group of Northwestern University students did a delightful version of Kipling's *The Elephant's Child,* designed after Paul Klee, with a selection of simple instruments to accent, underscore, and intensify the scenes. The rhythmic patterns of the sound effects complemented the stylized design.

These exercises are designed for teams within a large group. The observers for all exercises sit with their backs to the teams making the sounds. They are not to look at the sound source, so that we concentrate on reviving (from the golden age of radio) the skill of "seeing" with our ears.

Exercise #7—Team of 5 to 8 Players

Prepare a sound sequence that will reveal the following: Place (interior or exterior), time of day, weather conditions, what action takes place. Use no words. Create vocal sound effects, or add anything contained in the room to make appropriate sounds (knocking on wood, crumpling paper, opening doors, wastebasket tom-tom, etc.). Prepare in 5 minutes.

Observers: What took place? What was the time? Where did it happen? What was the weather? What sounds transmitted useful information?

Exercise #8—Rotate, New Teams of 5 Players

Tell a story (original) using vocal sounds but no words. Set a time, place, and mood. The walking sounds from Chapter VI may be used, as well as these substitutes for speech:

Ouuu	Harumph	Ouch
Ah-ha	Wow	Eek
Oh-ho	Yikes	Shhhh
Yoo-hoo	Scream	Grrrr

Continue the list with the "Breath of Life" sounds from Chapter VI.

Observers: What could you "see"? How did you discover the who, what, where, when, and how of each group?

Exercise #9—Rotate, New Teams of 5 to 8 Players

Select a well-known fairy tale. Select one or two scenes so that all players participate. Create original voice characterizations for each role. Retain the sex of the characters in the story, but cast the roles without always matching the sex of the players. Your purpose is to project "images" of the characters, as well as information on the time, place, period, mood, and weather. Prepare in 15 minutes, and share.

Observers: Describe the characters and settings as you saw them. What design images did the voices bring to mind? Was each character sharply defined? What emotions were expressed during the scene?

This chapter has focused on the puppeteer as the voice for varied disguises. The voice and action must now be focused into a single illusion for the larger purpose of achieving a characterization.

Chapter VIII

CHARACTERIZATION

To characterize is to identify the qualities that make one person or thing different from every other of its type. Our differences set us apart and make us unique. The source of these differences begins inside, in the way we think and feel about things, and extends to the outside in the way we move and speak.

The person without theatre training may find characterization a puzzling business. We spend our lives "just being ourselves." We have no occasion "to be somebody else" except for those fleeting moments when we do a take-off on someone who has amused or angered us. Then we find it easy to imitate another person's voice and mannerisms to make a point. It is this fleeting start that can be a springboard into what characterization is, and what to do to develop it.

These simplified steps may help to clarify the process.

Observation. Study other people. Note the walk, posture, voice, mannerisms, age, reactions, rhythms, habits, etc.

Imitation. Attempt to reproduce the "externals" of the observed character.

Identification. Now try to get "inside" the character by imagining the inner thoughts and feelings. One may be called upon to act a part quite opposite from his/her own personality. Discover the similarities in your thinking and feeling; understand the differences. Use both to build the image.

Selection. After generating a great deal of information, through observation and identification, it is time to choose those elements that are the essence of the character. The selective process should refine and simplify the internal/external view of the character without reducing it to a stereotype.

Invention. To the above steps, actors add something of their own imagination, and the composite—part truth, part fiction—becomes a characterization with theatrical validity.

Actors and puppeteers who work from a known quantity, the written play, will find that the playwright has provided clues to characterization in the script: the lines the character says; the lines that other characters say about him or her; the manner in which the thoughts and feelings are revealed or concealed in each scene; and the action each character takes in response to plot situations.

The success of villains in children's plays may be the result of playwright and actor teaming up to give that role the strongest and best characterization. In that durable classic *Hansel and Gretel,* children often find the Witch the most appealing character because she has the most life, zest, and pizzazz. The father is just a man; the mother is just a woman; Hansel and Gretel are just children. They are all blah. They all move the same way; they all speak the same way. There is no evidence of thinking or feeling in this robot family. Not one of them has an ounce of character, whereas the Witch is loaded with it. She *is* different! No wonder our sympathies are with the Witch who would remove these dull, unimaginative creatures by turning them into something as worthwhile as gingerbread. (Remember, the good guys need characterization too!)

The puppeteer with a variety act has the least need for characterization. A music tempo sets the beat, the act is brisk, the routines are short, there is no dialogue, and no time to build a character. The personality of the puppeteer seen on stage is a large part of the theatrical effect. The winning grin, the wink to the audience that asks, "Did you see that?" or "What do you think?" or "How'm I doin'—all right?" are methods of putting the act across. It is known as showmanship. The variety performer is somewhat like an acrobat, displaying dexterity and mastery of movement. It is the ability to do some trick, some bit of business that "sells" the act—the speed of the skater, the precision and glee of the juggler, the daring flips of the man on the flying trapeze—puppet feats done with bravado. Occationally a flash of personality appears in the puppet mime to music.

I would like to mention several of the variety and concert artists who have developed memorable characterizations. Cedric Head was a master at manipulating his favorite marionette, a teddy bear named Bruin. On stage Bruin received his instructions from Beppo the clown, but sometimes Head would bring Bruin out to show his friends, and then he spoke directly as a kindly ringmaster might to the star of the show. Bruin was a bit on the lazy, but lovable, side. After paddling into position, Bruin would sit down to rest and eye the audience in a winning way with a cock of his head. You could tell that Bruin thought that his just being there was enough. When he was asked to do his trick, he would shake his head as if he were too tired to consider it. After some coaxing, the bear could be persuaded to pick up a long bar and hold it out with his two paws. After a word of praise from Beppo (or Head), Bruin would slam the bar to the floor, sit down with a thump, and gaze happily at the audience as if it were all over. There was more to come, of course, and more cajoling to get Bruin to stand again, lift the bar, place it on his nose, drop his hands, and balance it carefully—carefully—whooooa, you almost dropped it there, easy now—and the bar would teeter precariously with every turn of the head until Bruin would sneeze, and the act would collapse. Watching the delight of the puppeteer in the antics of this personable bear was as much fun as watching Bruin himself. There was also a time out, while Bruin was

allowed to scratch a particular itch that had bothered him. The finale was a flash finish, wherein Bruin was allowed to lie flat on his back and balance the bar in the air on his toes. Cedric Head elevated the standard juggling act to a classic with his characterization of Bruin.

Albrecht Roser's concert evening includes a number of poignant and compelling mime characterizations. He has a comic Old Lady, who sits in a rocking chair knitting furiously between topical remarks. When the audience laughs, the Old Lady stops knitting, fixes her eyes out front, and tops the laugh with a sharp retort. The timing and the economy of movement—saved for just the right moments—keep the audience convulsed.

In his nightclub act Barclay Shaw uses a (marionette) chicken, which has the misfortune to lay an egg on stage. When the audience reacts with surprise, the chicken launches into a hilarious monologue on the trials and tribulations of being a chicken in the first place. Each audience response spurs the chicken into further asides, ad libs, and embellishments to build the characterization along with the laughter.

Jay Marshall works with an unusual rabbit named Lefty. Lefty is created out of a white gloved hand, two eyes, two ears, and a mouth formed by the hollow space created when the end of the thumb touches the end of the index finger. Lefty has no body, but he does have character. With his flexible mouth and unflappable wit, Lefty is able to spar with Marshall to keep the audience in stitches.

Walton & O'Rourke, the team that created the animated hand puppets for *Lili,* toured the international show places with their famed marionettes. Their setup provided an elevated stage for the marionettes, and the operators were visible over the waist-high backdrop. For their routine with Madam Bussbottom, Michael O'Rourke appeared in person as the waiter to fetch and carry chair, table, and drinks for this grand dame's excursion into café society. When the Madam arrived, she surveyed the crowd, demanded a table, and asked the waiter to assist her in being seated.

Madam Bussbottom, the blueblood from Lower Basin Street, by Walton and O'Rourke.

Charlie Chaplin, a lollipop puppet (face mask on stick). Marionette Theatre Arts Council, Pittsburgh; Margo Lovelace.

Cincinnati puppeteer Larry Smith with ventriloquist figure.

Lady Ann of Richard III, *in "Excerpts from Shakespeare," by the National Theatre of Puppet Arts.*

After calling for a menu, she surveyed the drink list carefully through her lorgnette. It was soon apparent that this blueblood from Lower Basin Street was one to be reckoned with, and she intended to have a night on the town. She ordered a cocktail and fussed until it was put down on the table in front of her. She sipped it through a straw until the glass was drained dry, humming softly to herself. She called for the waiter and ordered another. Several drinks later, Madam Bussbottom was losing control—she called raucously for the waiter, demanded attention, burped through her tirade, and wondered why her hairdo was beginning to fall down. The waiter tried to be civil but asked her to leave. When she refused, he whisked away the table and chair, and the unsteady Madam B. fell flat on her backside. It was a moment to remember, hilarious and touching at the same time. It was like seeing a favorite friend in an embarrassing situation, and it happened because of the captivating characterization of the lady who had too much, too soon.

The puppeteers who have most need for characterization are those who invent a cast of characters in the "commedia" style. (See *Court and Commedia* in the *Theatre Student* series.) These characters must be consistent and remain the same throughout various episodes and adventures. The puppeteer serves as "playwright-in-residence" to the cast by knowing every thought, move, feeling, and word before it appears on the stage. This thorough rapport between the puppeteer-creator and the puppet-character-identity results in the creation of originals, those one-of-a-kind beings that no other performer could duplicate.

In this category we would place Edgar Bergen and Charlie McCarthy, Burr Tillstrom with Kukla, Ollie, and all the Kuklapolitans, Shari Lewis and Lamb Chop, and Jim Henson and Kermit. These artists have left their personal stamp on puppetry, as Chaplin, Marcel Marceau, Mae West, Mickey Mouse and Donald Duck, and Charlie Brown and Snoopy have in their respective fields.

It is interesting to note that the walk-around Disney figures are not allowed to speak. They may move as Mickey Mouse or Pluto, but the persons inside are not entrusted with the thoughts, the feelings, and the voices of these characters, and so they must remain silent. This may explain why puppeteers are sensitive about having other people handle their puppets. Outsiders cannot understand the roles, for they have not lived with, thought for, and spoken through these disguises. No one can assume the same sensitivity toward the characters as their creator. The puppet is not only the ultimate disguise, but also an intimate disguise where no trespassing is allowed.

Characterization is the process by which the puppeteer identifies those thoughts and feelings that will be expressed in the voice and movement characterization of the puppet to make it delightfully different from all others.

Exercise #1—Opposites, 2 Puppeteers

An easy way to start building characterization is by playing a game of opposites, so that each puppet has the maximum contrast in character. Many ventriloquists use this method to separate themselves from the character of the dummy. Select one of the combinations below and develop a scene between those two characters.

young/old	stingy/generous
sick/well	goofy/serious
lazy/energetic	sweet/sour
bold/shy	happy/sad
sexy/sedate	

Reflection: Did one character tend to fall into a "straight" role as a foil for the other character, or were both equal?

Exercise #2—Thinking, 1 Puppeteer

Develop a pantomime for a puppet character. How can the puppet show us everything it is thinking without dialogue? All the thoughts and actions should be consistent for the same character.

Reflection: What was the puppet thinking? What kind of character did the observers see?

Exercise #3—Feeling, 1 Puppeteer

Develop a pantomime to show what the puppet feels without dialogue. Can the puppet recover from one feeling and move on to another?

Reflection: What feelings were expressed through the puppet action? What character emerged?

Exercise #4—Provoke Emotion, 2 Puppeteers

Devise a scene for two puppets, using voices and movements, in which Puppet A tries to provoke Puppet B into a strong expression of emotion (love, hate, fear, etc.). Build the scene a step at a time until the emotion grows in Puppet B and bursts forth. Have Puppet B recover composure and calm down, with or without help from Puppet A.

Example: The town rascal flirts with an old maid, becoming more and more romantic as she resists. When he asks her to say she loves him, the old maid does so with a passion. How does he/she/they get out of it?

Exercise #5—Generation and Gender, 1 Puppeteer, 2 Puppets

One puppeteer is to develop a scene using two characters, one of them to be the opposite gender of the puppeteer, and one the same. Each puppet character should be in a different generation. Take time to develop the characters and the situation that brings them together.

Reflection for Puppeteer: How did it feel to play two different roles at the same time? Was one character easier to act than the other? What part of the character did you build from observation, from identification, from invention?

Chapter IX

PUPPET CONSTRUCTION

Building a puppet is a unique experience. During the construction process, the builder begins to identify with the object. By the time the puppet is completed, a working partnership is in progress. The end product, the puppet, is more than a jointed doll or a controllable sculpture. It is an instrument for projecting character. The creator provides the signs of life; the puppet provides the right disguise.

Directions for making four simple puppets are included here. The finger puppet and the hand puppet are operated from inside; the rod puppet and the string puppet are controlled from the outside. Our objective is not to build the most beautiful nor the most perfect puppet, but rather to introduce the reader to a working model of each type. The essentials of each figure are reduced to the simplest form that can be constructed in the least amount of time. Shortcuts have been suggested by using pre-formed shapes or ready-made substitutes. The emphasis is on *using* the puppet, not on perfecting its appearance the first time around. Directions for more sophisticated methods of construction can be found in the fine books on puppet-making listed in the Bibliography.

GENERAL INSTRUCTIONS

Planning

Start with a character idea. Use it to make decisions about the puppet you are going to build. Beginners will find that a rough sketch helps to visualize the finished puppet.

Design to Scale

The rod puppet and the marionette will require a full-scale drawing to indicate:

a) overall height of figure. (Standard sizes for a string puppet, representing a 6' adult, are 18″, 24″, and 36″ based on scales of 3″, 4″, and 6″ = 1 foot.)
b) relative proportions of head, torso, hands, limbs.
c) points where joints are intended, so that these distances can be measured to develop patterns for individual sections.

Patterns and Templates

Patterns can be made of newspaper, brown kraft paper, construction paper, or tracing paper.

The hand-puppet body pattern may require more than one try. Save the original pattern, study it for problem areas, and make revisions to develop a satisfactory fit for your hand.

When a pattern outline is to be traced many times, a template of lightweight cardboard is useful.

A single pattern will do for hands or feet, but remember to flip it over to trace a right side and a left side.

Transferring Pattern Outlines to Materials

I use a ball-point pen to trace patterns on the reverse side of fabric. The traced line is the *exact stitching line*. A seam allowance of ¼″ to ½″ must be added outside the marked line.

Xavier de Callatay, designer, and Nancy Staub, director, with one of the large rod puppets requiring two manipulators for Garcia-Lorca's The Love of Don Perlimplin for Belissa in the Garden. *The production was by the Puppet Playhouse for the New Orleans Museum of Art, 1974.*

A nylon-tip pen leaves the best marking on styrofoam and foam rubber.

Tools and Materials

A supply list is provided for each puppet project. After constructing these trial figures to discover their action potential, you may wish to build others of each type using other construction methods and materials. Your personal style of puppetry will grow out of the choices you make.

Time

I have watched one well-known puppeteer whack out·a new puppet character in a day of intense activity. Another puppeteer tinkers with a single puppet for several weeks. We hope these instructions will allow you to build a workable puppet in a few sessions, so that you can move along to rehearsing with it.

FINGER PUPPET (*See Fig. 1*)

Step 1. In this version of the finger puppet (A), the head and feet are not permanently

attached, so that other heads and shoes could be substituted to create new characters.

Tools:
ball-point pen.
sewing needle.
sewing machine.
scissors.
Magic Marker or nylon-tip pen.
stuffing stick (blunt end of pencil or rounded end of a ½″ dowel).
glue brush.

Materials:
flexible cardboard for ankle tubes: light posterboard, cereal box, or laundry shirt card, manila folder.
unbleached muslin for feet and ankle covering.
stuffing material: filler cotton, dacron filler, or kapok.

Finger puppet sequence for Northeastern Wisconsin In-School Telecommunications program on Creative Drama, University of Wisconsin–Green Bay. Eileen Littig, producer; Barry Stoner, director; George Latshaw, puppeteer.

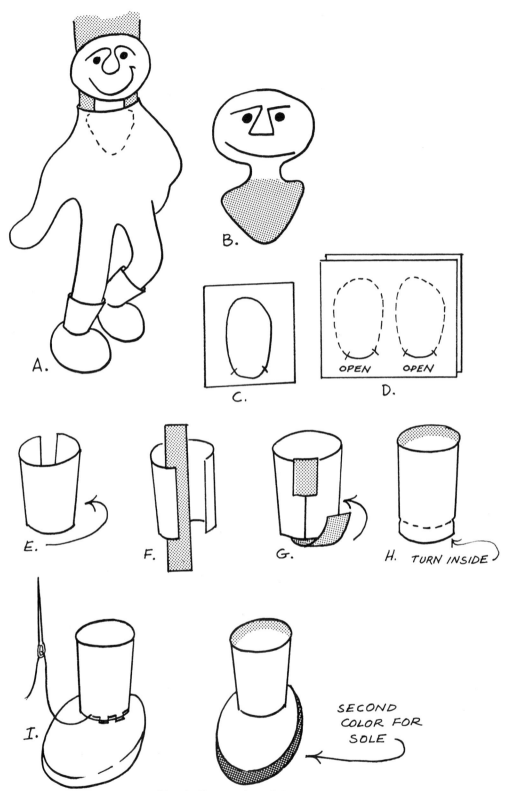

FIG. *1. Construction of finger puppet.*

masking tape ½″ or ¾″ wide.

white glue (Elmer's glue).

1 fabric glove: cotton work glove, garden glove, or white lisle film editor's glove (cotton knit).

Step 2. Design *Head* (B) shape and cut it out of light cardboard; include tab below neck (shaded area) to tuck inside top of glove to hold head upright. Draw features on face with Magic Marker.

Step 3. Body—Any sort of soft, snug-fitting fabric glove will do. The back of the hand is the front of the body. In this model, the thumb sticks out at one side to simulate an arm. Index and middle fingers are legs; ring & little fingers are tucked back out of sight.

Step 4. Feet/Shoes—Make a paper pattern (C) for shoe approximately 2″ long. Trace outline on muslin for one right and one left shoe. Stitch together two layers of fabric for each shoe (D). Leave an unstitched opening in back, so the seam can be turned inside before stuffing. (One layer of fabric might be another color of cotton or felt, to make a muslin "upper," and a colored sole.) Fill shoe with stuffing material. Use blunt end of pencil or pen as stuffing stick to pack cotton filler firmly into the shape. Hand-sew seam closed at the back.

Step 5. Ankle—Cut two strips of cardboard 1″ wide by 5″ long. Curl cardboard strips by pulling over table edge, or by wrapping around wooden dowel. Strips should curl easily without cracking.

Step 5a. From the curled paper, shape two tubes large enough to fit over index and middle fingers. These tubes are tapered slightly toward the bottom, so the fingers wearing the glove can be wedged inside (in the manner of wearing a thimble.) Tension keeps the feet on the gloved fingers. If the tubes are too loose, the feet may fly off during a vigorous dance.

Step 5b. Mark and cut each cardboard strip to fit, so that edges butt together neatly with no overlap (E).

Step 5c. Join two vertical edges together with strip of masking tape, first sealing inside edges together (F).

Step 5d. Fold remaining tape down to seal outside seam (G).

Step 6. Glue a muslin covering on each tube, allowing an extra ½″ to extend top and bottom. Finish top edge by gluing overlap to inside of tube (H). Turn bottom muslin edge to inside of tube without gluing; this soft fabric edge is needed to sew the ankle to the stuffed foot.

Step 7. When muslin cover has dried, sew base of tube (ankle) to stuffed foot. Use double #50 thread. Pull knotted end through foot where it will not show. Take one stitch in top layer; place next stitch in bottom layer; alternate all around (I). If stitches are placed close together the sewing will not show, and the two pieces will be joined securely.

Now assemble the pieces. Put on glove; tuck tab end of head into glove; press index and middle fingers into the ankle tubes. Put the finger puppet through the routine of being:

A square dancer	An ice skater
A karate kicker	A tightrope walker
A can-can dancer	A trampoline whiz

HAND PUPPET (See Fig. 2)

A simple rehearsal puppet (A) can be made using a 4″ styrofoam ball for the head, a short length of plastic water pipe for the neck (also called fingerstall), and a work glove or unbleached muslin garment for the body. The construction process is divided into three sections, Heads, Bodies, Hands.

Head

Step 1.

Materials:

4″ styrofoam ball.

wooden bead, or drawer pull (nose).

¼″ dowel (short length) or wooden meat skewer to fit inside nose as plug extension.

1′ of black plastic water pipe (¾″ or 1″ internal diameter); PVC (polyvinyl chloride) pipe available from building supply dealer, hardware store, or lumberyard.

B. ALTER THE BALL SHAPE

C. NOSES WITH INSERT PLUGS

CARDBOARD PLUG

SLASH EDGES & PRESS DOWN

MASKING TAPE

D.

BEVEL WALL OF TUBING

E. CROSS SECTION

SAW TOOTH CUTTING EDGE

F.

A.

MUSLIN COVER + FELT LEDGE

G.

THE SECOND JOINT OF INDEX FINGER

H.

Fig. 2. *Construction of hand puppet.*

cardboard.

masking tape.

unbleached muslin.

fine sandpaper.

Elmer's glue.

⅜″ strip of felt.

Tools:

coping saw or small keyhole saw.

utility knife.

pencil sharpener.

scissors and glue brush (10¢ acid brush from hardware store).

Step 2. You may want to alter the shape of the styrofoam ball (B) by slicing off a segment to flatten the face or the top of the head. Use saw to cut styrofoam; then use sandpaper to smooth the sawed surface.

Step 3. Nose—Fit dowel or wooden skewer into hole of nose shape (C). Allow 1″ to extend, and cut off at this length. Use a pencil sharpener to shape one end of dowel to a point. Glue flat end of dowel into hole in nose. Poke pointed end into styrofoam head. May be glued in place if you wish.

Step 4. Neck (fingerstall)—Choose size of plastic water pipe (¾″ or 1″ diameter) so index finger can slip in as far as second joint without being wedged. The finger should be able to turn slightly inside the tube. Saw a piece 3″ long. Trim sawed edges smooth with utility knife. Cut a cardboard circle to form a cap for top of plastic tube. Fasten in place with masking tape (first place cap on top, wrap tape around tube, slash top half of masking tape to form tabs) and then press tabs down on top.

Step 5. Cutting tool—With remaining 9″ piece of pipe, fashion a homemade cutting tool for styrofoam, which will make a hole the exact size of the neck tube. Bevel the inside walls of one end of the pipe (E). Use utility knife so that walls taper out to a fine edge. Notch beveled edge in sawtooth pattern all around (F). The "cutter" is now ready to use.

Step 6. Make a hole 1½″ deep in styrofoam head to receive neck section. Push and twist cutter to that depth in styrofoam; pull out sharply. A plug of styrofoam should be re-

moved with cutter. If it does not release, carefully pry or slice plug out with knife. Do not enlarge walls of neck hole in the process.

Step 7. Coat capped top and 1½″ sides of plastic neck tube with Elmer's glue. Drop Elmer's glue in styrofoam head hole—spread with brush. Insert neck tube into head, capped end first. Glue a muslin cover around exposed plastic pipe section of neck. Glue felt strip around base of neck to form wall or ledge (G). Coat both sides of felt with glue before wrapping around, and use brush to coat finished wall. (This will harden surface.) Felt should wrap around at least three times to form wall.

Step 8. The finger stall should extend down to the second joint of the index finger (H). If it slips below this point, poke cotton or soft stuffing in to fill top of neck tube, so that neck stays at right level. The second finger joint forms base for important head action, and must be free.

Body (Undergarment) (See Fig. 3.)

An unbleached muslin underbody will absorb moisture to keep puppet costumes looking fresher. This garment should fit snugly as a base for whatever costume follows. It should feel comfortable on either right or left hand, even though the thumb and middle finger (puppet arms) are not equally spaced on puppeteers' hand.

Step 1.

Materials:

pattern paper.

unbleached muslin.

3 small pieces of chamois (could be from pieced skin).

#50 cotton sewing thread.

pins.

ball-point pen or tailor's chalk pencil.

1½″ curtain ring.

heavy-duty carpet thread, or button thread.

Elmer's glue.

Tools:

scissors.

sewing machine.

sewing needle.

large-eyed needle for heavy thread.

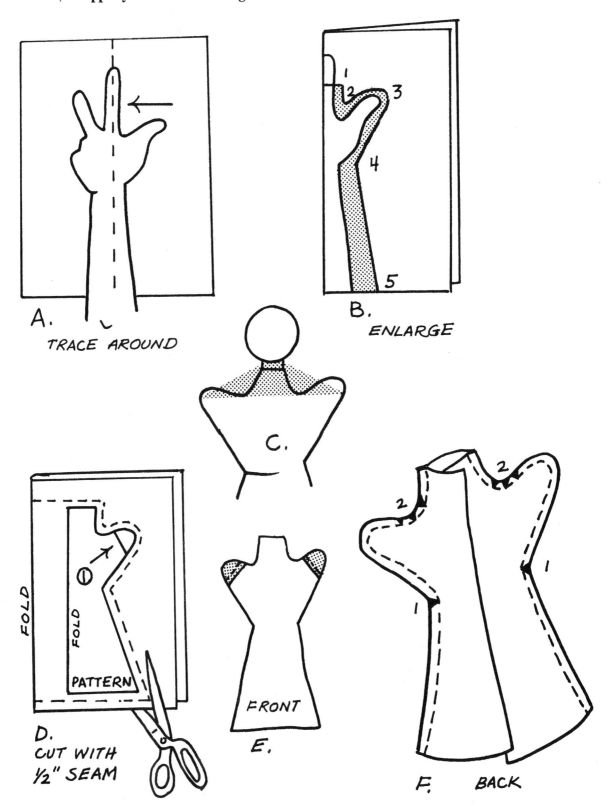

A. TRACE AROUND

B. ENLARGE

C.

D. CUT WITH ½" SEAM

E. FRONT

F. BACK

Fig. 3. *Construction of underbody for hand puppet.*

Step 2. To make a pattern, take a piece of paper the length of your arm and a bit wider than the span of your fingers. Fold it in half lengthwise to obtain a center line. Open out paper and center your left hand on fold with fingers spread in hand puppet position (A). Loosely trace around fingers and forearm. Mark position of index finger's second joint on drawing. Note unequal division of bulk between two sides. Pattern adjustments are made on the thumb side to compensate for higher position of middle finger, and also to accommodate thickness of hand (B). Mark top of pattern—the line of the index finger second joint (B1). Start 1 or 1½ inches from the fold to enlarge outline for pattern. Do not dip down into hollow of thumb (B2), but retain a slight upward angle in tracing around to thumb side (B3). Widen angle down to waist (the wrist) (B4), and flare out to bottom of garment (B5). (A wide base makes it easier to get hand in and out of the puppet.) Fold pattern and cut along adjusted outline so both sides of pattern are the same. You will see when pattern is opened out that you have cut off the middle finger of original tracing. Do not panic. The body will be made in fabric, which will adjust to finger positions. The design you have made is for the size of the *front* of the body only!

An Aside to the Reader: Most hand-puppet patterns show a loose shape that is the same front and back. The problem with this type of body is that there is too much bulk in the front to interfere with hand movements, and the garment is so loose that the puppet hands slip off the fingertips during the first broad gesture. Since puppet arms can extend no further than a 180° angle, seam lines should fit snugly around fingertips in this position. When body is attached to head, there should be a triangle of tension (Drawing C) between points C1, C2, and C3.

Step 3. Trace front body pattern on unbleached muslin with ball-point pen. Cut ½" outside marked line for seam allowance.

Step 4. Back Body Pieces—Fold a length of

JULIAN APSEL STUDIO

Natalie Hackenschmidt as the Miller's daughter in Rumplestiltskin. *George Latshaw puppets.*

muslin. Place folded body pattern about 2" away from fold with fold of pattern parallel to fold of material. Trace around outside outline of body pattern. Extend top and bottom lines over to fold. Cut ½" larger than traced line (for seam allowance) through both layers of material (D). Turn folded cut-out material over, and trace body pattern outline on that side. Slit material down center fold line. You now have a basic body in three pieces. As it is assembled, you will see that alterations can be made after side seams are sewed together by leaving this back seam open until the last.

Step 5. Two pieces of chamois will serve as the "palms" of the hands. The slightly rough texture provides a secure grip in handling props, and the extra thickness withstands the wear of handling props, clapping, rubbing, etc.

A single layer of muslin would wear out in short order.

Mark a 1″ section from the tip of the thumb side of pattern (D1). Trace this outline on a piece of chamois. Cut right and left outlines with ½″ extra seam allowance.

Step 6. Place front body section in front of you with unmarked side up. (This will be the right side of the material.) Place a chamois pad over palm on each side, rounded edges matching the muslin. Machine stitch chamois to muslin across straight line at the base of pad only (E). Now place two back body sections on top of front section, right sides together. The traced pattern outlines should be on the outside of both top and bottom. Machine stitch each side seam together using pattern line as the exact stitching line. This side seam locks the rest of chamois pad insert in place. The chamois seam allowance can be clipped to within ⅛ inch of stitching if it seems too bulky. Without turning seams, slip your fingers into the arm sections to see if there is a bit of tension across front of garment when arms are extended. A bit of instant tailoring can improve the fit, if necessary.

Step 7. Before moving on, clip the seams (F), at points F1 at the waist, and also in about three places around the curve at F2. If seams are not clipped (almost to stitching), the work will pucker when it is turned right side out. If you have a knack for sewing, this is the time to steam-press open the seams so the work will lie flat.

Step 8 (See Fig. 4). If seam lines do not feel completely snug against fingertips, use two darts to take up some of the excess in the front of the body. The first is a half-moon dart across the waist from A1 to A2. With the body spread open, seam side up, fold body in half at the waist. Mark and machine sew a half-moon dart (B1–2) from side seam to side seam only. Open the work, and you will see that the body bends forward slightly at the waist. Now fold body in half along the vertical front center line. Mark and sew dart C3–4. Do not sew beyond waistline dart. Slip your hand inside to see if front stays snug.

Step 9. Sew the back seam. Turn up a hem. The finished puppet should be slightly shorter than the inside elbow bend of the puppeteer's forearm. Base of costume should move freely when manipulating hand turns it left or right. Machine sew hem.

Step 10. The finishing touch is the reinforcing patch of chamois, which is sewed inside the body, covering the back seam just above the hem (D). Note pattern of stitching, all around edges of the square, and criss-cross the middle. Sew curtain ring just below center of chamois square. Use carpet thread, doubled, and do not pull stitches too tight, so there is a slight play in the ring, which should extend slightly below garment. This point of the body receives a great deal of stress in hanging position while puppeteer is getting in and out of puppet.

Step 11. Use marked line at top of body (neck section) to make big running stitches with single carpet thread (E). This will act as a drawstring. Crease seam back, so that running stitches lie on top of fold. Apply glue to base of puppet head, all around top and sides of the projecting lip. Carefully center muslin body neck section over puppet head neck. Press front center in place and pull drawstring, easing fullness to sides and back of garment around neck. Tie drawstring tightly, so it could not pull off the ledge of neck.

HAND SANDWICH (See Fig. 5.)

A simple cartoon-type hand with flexible fingers can be made with a felt and foam sandwich.

Step 1.
Materials:
  flesh-colored felt.
  contrasting color artfoam.
  cardboard hand pattern.
Tools:
  ball-point pen (red) for tracing hand pattern.
  scissors.
  sewing machine.
  #50 thread and needle for hand stitching.
Step 2. Make a hand pattern of lightweight

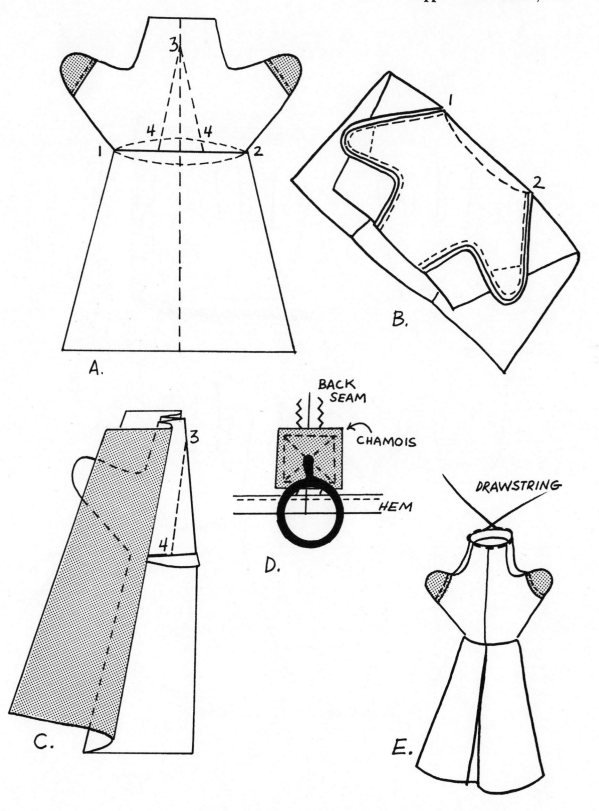

FIG. 4. *Details of hand puppet body.*

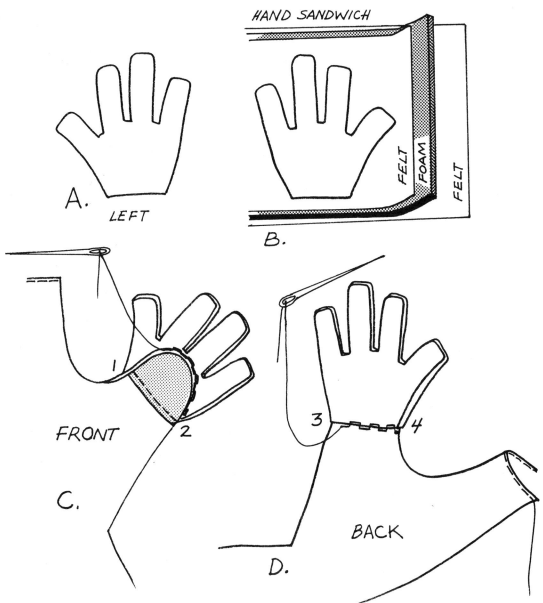

FIG. 5. *Construction of a hand sandwich.*

cardboard. Draw with thumb and four fingers or, cartoon-style, with thumb and three fingers, allowing enough space between fingers for seam allowance when cut apart. Trace right and left hand on one layer of felt (A).

Step 3. Assemble sandwich with bottom layer of felt, middle layer of colored art foam, and top layer of felt with outline drawn on it. Machine stitch the tracing of hand and fingers on all sides (through 3 layers of "sandwich"). Cut out each hand, leaving ⅛″ seam allowance outside stitching. Felt will not ravel, so the narrower allowance is safe (B).

Step 4. Hand sew the hand sandwich to puppet body. Thumb and fingers extend beyond the chamois palm and are placed in back of second layer of garment (C). Stitch felt hand to edge of muslin seam around curve (C 1–2) first, rather than try to sew through chamois. Then sew bottom of hand to back layer of garment (D). Be sure to catch stitches in back layer only, or you will have sewed shut the "pocket" where your fingertips should be.

The hand puppet is now ready to go through the exercises listed in Chapter VI, *Images in Action.* When it has been through all the movement games, it can be rewarded with a "makeup" and a suggestion of costume. Cut features and ears of felt or colored construction paper and pin in place. Add a wig or hat when the puppet has earned the right to these visual aids to performance.

ROD PUPPET (See Fig. 6)

The central rod (spine) supports the figure and controls head action. Rods attached to each hand articulate the jointed arms. In a true rod puppet, the puppeteer forms no part of the anatomy; the main support rod extends below the puppet and all manipulation is from the outside. This illustration (A) is actually a hand-and-rod puppet, developed in the mid-1940's by Marjorie Batchelder, Vivian Michael, and Gayle Michael (Anderson) for improvising plays with junior high school and college students. The human hand inside provides a flexible waist, and a muscular vitality to the body movement. A costume of draped fabric will conceal the half-human, half-wooden anatomy inside.

Step 1.

Materials:

1 piece of white sheet styrofoam 5″ x 12″ x 2″ thick (for head, neck, nose). Standard sheet size 1′ x 3′ x 2″.

several 6″ wood applicator sticks (thin sticks for cotton swabs available at drug stores).

1 short length of 1⅜″ lattice (shoulders).

1 ½″ dowel approximately 6″ to 8″ long (spine).

1 2′ length of ½″ half round (2 arms).

2 ¼″-diameter x 3′ wooden dowels (arm rods).

medium galvanized wire.

sandpaper.

venetian blind cord (or comparable sturdy, woven, flexible cord).

1 ½″-diameter x 9″ piece of copper tubing (plumbing supply).

colored felt and artfoam for hand sandwich construction.

Rehearse first! Apply character makeup last.

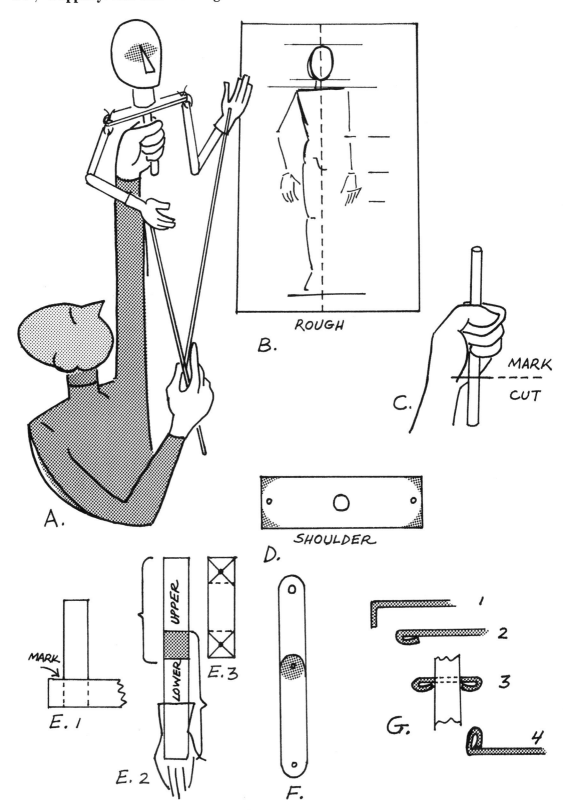

B. ROUGH

C. MARK CUT

D. SHOULDER

A.

E. 1 MARK

E. 2 LOWER UPPER

E. 3

F.

G. 1 2 3 4

Fig. 6. *Construction of a rod puppet.*

Elmer's glue (white glue).

masking tape ¾" wide.

soft knit fabric for draping costume (old dyed T-shirts).

art tissue paper in colors.

wheat paste (wallpaper paste dry) and small bowl for mixing.

pattern paper and marking pencil.

Tools:

drill with assorted small bits up to ½".

needle-nose wire-cutter pliers.

awl or drawing compass (for point).

coping saw or small keyhole saw.

utility knife.

hacksaw.

shoemaker's rasp, 8" long, one half-round and one flat side, with both rough and fine cuts on each side.

scissors.

cheap 1" paintbrush for wheat paste work.

sewing needle and thread.

Step 2. Scale Drawing. On a large piece of paper, rough out the size of the rod puppet. Mark a vertical center line; take it from the top and work down. Head 5" long, neck 2" long, make horizontal line to indicate shoulders. Make a fist; place fist and forearm over center line just underneath shoulder. Mark distance to wrist. Mark distance down to 3" short of elbow. Draw horizontal base line there. Mark width of shoulders. Rough in a torso, from shoulders to waist to hip, and leg line down to base. With this loose body outline in view, it is easy to mark the length of arms and hands, with elbow joint at the waist level (B).

Step 3. Mark and Cut Pieces.

Spine. Measure 3" from end of ½" dowel, and mark. Grip dowel in left hand (below the mark), and mark other end the length needed for hand grip plus 1". Saw off excess; round off end with knife; sand smooth (C).

Shoulders. Mark width of shoulders on piece of 1⅜" lattice. Saw piece to size. Round off all four corners of shoulder. Sand corners and edges smooth (D).

Upper Arms. Mark shoulder to elbow length on ½" half round. Saw two pieces this length.

Lower Arm and Palm. Place piece of half round at right angles to upper arm section; mark. Start length of lower arm measurement from this mark (E1) down to end of palm of hand. This overlap (shaded area E2) is necessary for wire pin joint. Cut two lower arm sections of half round.

Step 4. Mark and Drill Holes.

Spine. Use awl to start hole at 3" mark. Drill hole the size of wire. (Heavier coat-hanger wire could be substituted here.)

Shoulder. Mark center and drill ½" hole; sand smooth. Spine dowel must be able to slip through hole and turn easily. At each side of shoulder, mark a center ¼" in from edge. Drill holes large enough for venetian-blind cord to pass through. Sand smooth.

Upper Arms. Mark square at top end of arm (overlap method). Draw lines from opposite corners of square to find center point where lines intersect. Start hole with awl. Drill hole the size of venetian-blind cord in both pieces. Mark these ends "top." Find centers on other end (each piece), mark and drill holes the size of galvanized wire.

Lower Arms. Repeat. Mark centers for holes at each end of each piece. Drill holes the size of galvanized wire.

Control Rods. Carefully drill hole size of galvanized wire ¼" from end of each hand control rod (¼" x 3' dowel).

Step 5. Finish Arms. Round off both ends of each arm section. Sand smooth. Test joint by running wire through upper and lower arm overlap at elbow joint (flat surfaces together). Parts should swing freely. There should be no projecting section at elbow as arm bends.

Step 6. Method of Bending Wire to Form Pin Joints

Spine. This pin can be made of coat-hanger wire, since it is both the stop and the support for shoulders. Bend about ½" end of wire at right angles. Continue to bend this section back on itself. Pinch as flat as possible (G1 and G2). Run free end of wire through hole in dowel. Allow 1″ to extend. Clip off excess. Bend another ½″ loop back on itself (G3) to seal pin in place. It is important to have each loop butt into dowel, so the pin cannot slip back and forth in hole, changing balance of shoulder support.

Elbows. The lighter galvanized wire is easier to bend in a flat loop. It is also bent one more time (G4) so it is parallel to arm sections. In this position it will not catch on costumes. Make pin joints for each elbow, so arms swing freely.

Step 7. Assemble String Joint. Run a short length of venetian-blind cord through hole in upper arm. Pass one end up through hole in shoulder. Tie ends off in square knot, so upper arm hangs loose from shoulder and can move in any direction. Curved section of the half round faces in toward body; flat section faces out. Coat knot with Elmer's glue to make it permanent. Check both arms to match length.

STYROFOAM HEAD (See Fig. 7)

Step 1. Design a simple head shape 4″ wide and 5″ long. (Refer to Chapter V.) Cut paper pattern of full front view (A).

Step 2. Trace pattern outline twice on styrofoam, and saw out both pieces with coping saw or small keyhole saw.

Step 3. Stack the two matching outlines of styrofoam to form 4" thick block. Use 3″ lengths of applicator sticks (sharpen one end to a point) or toothpicks to "nail" the two sections together at 4 points (B). These should be at least 1″ from outer edge. Drive each nail at slight angle toward center to lock halves together. Push each stick ½″ below surface of styrofoam.

Step 4. Mark a line 1″ in from edge around top and two sides on top of block. Mark 1″ line around side of block. Do not mark lower section (the chin).

Step 5. Use saw or rasp to make straight cut to remove all material between these two

markings (shaded area D). This is a fast method of shaping head, knocking off corners to move toward curved shape.

Step 6. Repeat marking and sawing for complete outline at back of head.

Step 7. Use fine cut of rasp or sandpaper to remove the remaining sharp edges (shaded area E). Sandpaper surface smooth.

Step 8. Cut a circle of styrofoam for neck. Place head atop neck to determine best angle. Top of neck can be planed forward to change head angle. Mark and match flat plane on head where it will join neck, so flat surfaces can be glued together.

Step 9. Shape a nose of styrofoam. Sand smooth.

Step 10. Glue nose and neck to the head with Elmer's glue (F). Reinforce nose by driving several of the applicator stick "nails" in to hold it to head. The neck is "nailed" in place at four points around the circle (G). The center must be free for the wooden dowel spine. Push all wooden sticks below surface of work.

Step 11. Make a cutting tool for styrofoam from the 9″ length of ½″-diameter copper tubing. Make a series of cuts ½″ deep around the circumference with a hacksaw. With pliers, bend and break away every other section, or saw away alternates (H).

Step 12. Holding head and neck firmly together, push and twist cutting tool to a depth of 2¾″. A sharp twist and pull will remove styrofoam plug. Spine dowel is glued in later.

PAPIER MÂCHÉ "SKINS" FOR STYROFOAM (See Fig. 7)

Three layers of art tissue papier mâché will protect the fragile surface of the styrofoam head at the same time they are adding color. The tissue paper is remarkably tough and resilient when dry and satisfactory for moderately hard use.

Step 1. Follow package directions for mixing wheat paste (hot- or cold-water mix). The dry powder is always added to water, a little

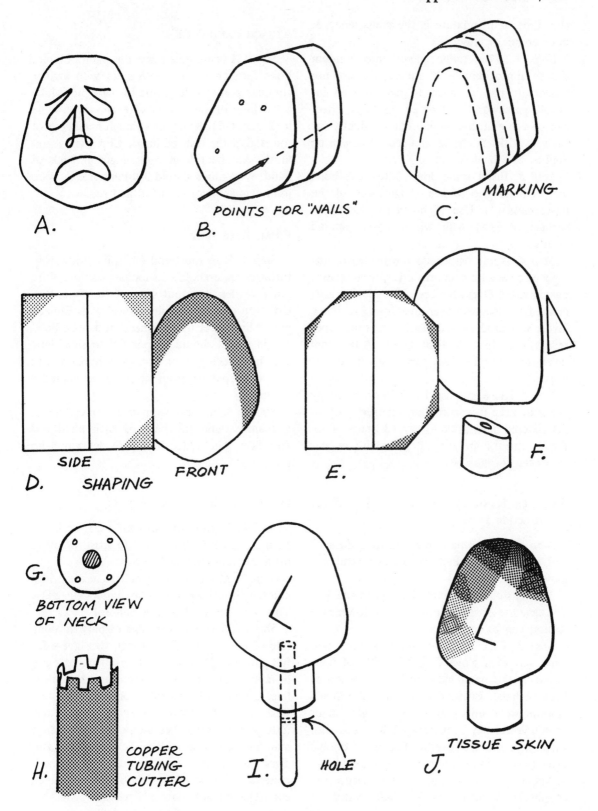

A.

B. POINTS FOR "NAILS"

C. MARKING

D. SIDE SHAPING FRONT

E.

F.

G. BOTTOM VIEW OF NECK

H. COPPER TUBING CUTTER

I. HOLE

J. TISSUE SKIN

Fig. 7. *Construction of styrofoam head.*

at a time, until mixture is the consistency of thick cream or gravy.

Step 2. Tear tissue paper into random shapes approximately 2″ square. Do not use scissors to cut. Torn edges melt into an invisible patchwork. A mottled "collage" effect can be achieved by varying colors slightly for each layer. Rosy cheeks and red noses can be applied as a final contrasting layer.

Step 3. Insert spine dowel into neck hole, use as hand grip to keep fingers out of the paste mess (I). Use 1″ brush to coat entire surface of head with wheat paste. Spread evenly.

Step 4. Apply tissue paper with brush, lifting a piece at a time on brush. Lay tissue down, paste over it. Overlap pieces. Note darker area created by the two-layer overlap (J). Three layers will produce a darker, even tone. Spot places you miss by light color. After final layer, smooth off excess paste with fingers or brush.

Step 5. Rinse out paste brush in warm, soapy water to keep it in condition for next project. Set covered head aside to dry 12 hours or so. Paper shrinks in drying and will appear smoother dry than wet.

ANOTHER HAND SANDWICH (See Fig. 5 for instructions)

Step 1. Make a pattern for hand. Add a 2″ cuff beyond wrist. Pattern should resemble a glove (Fig. 8A).

Step 2. Follow assembly instructions in Fig. 5. Leave top of glove unstitched, so lower arm section can be inserted.

Step 3. Glue lower arm-palm section into hand sandwich glove (B). Flat side of half-round is the palm side; rounded portion is back of hand. Brush light coating of Elmer's glue on wood only—avoid getting glue in or near hole for pin joint. Insert lower arm with single layer of felt covering flat palm; double layer (foam and felt) at back. Use carpet tacks or staple gun (as well as glue) to secure top of glove to wooden arm. Set aside to dry.

ATTACH HAND RODS

Step 1. Locate hole for pin in palm of hand. Poke through felt on both sides with awl or compass point to clear hole for wire pin. Make a flat loop of galvanized wire and right-angle it (Fig. 6, G4). Run wire through hand control rod and palm side of hand. Clip excess and finish with bent loop right angle at back of hand. Wire loops should not bind action. Wire joint acts as pivot for hand and rod.

FINAL ASSEMBLY

Step 1. Run short end of "spine" dowel up through center hole of shoulder section. Wire pin provides stop and support for shoulders. Coat top portion of spine dowel with Elmer's glue. Slip dowel up into head and neck hole. Pin in dowel should be parallel to shoulders, with head facing front. Lay work horizontal to dry to keep glue from dripping on shoulder section.

Step 3. Glue and wrap a 2″-wide strip of artfoam around the base of each hand rod (see 8C). The added bulk provides a nonslip grip.

DRAPE THE SHAPE (See Fig. 8)

Step 1. Spread arms straight out from body. Measure distance from wrist to wrist. Measure distance from shoulder to base.

Step 2. Make a paper pattern using width and length as points on a large arc (Fig. 8D). This view shows half the pattern.

Step 3. Place straight edge of pattern along fold of knit fabric. Cut through two layers for full garment. If necessary to use smaller piece of fabric, cut two pieces and seam at shoulder line. Cut small hole center for spine rod, and slash 5″ or 6″ down center of back. Carefully pull garment over puppet head. Arrange material across shoulders. Sew up back slit. Tack (sewing term for repeated small stitches) material to wrist. Knit fabric will not ravel; cut edges do not require a hem.

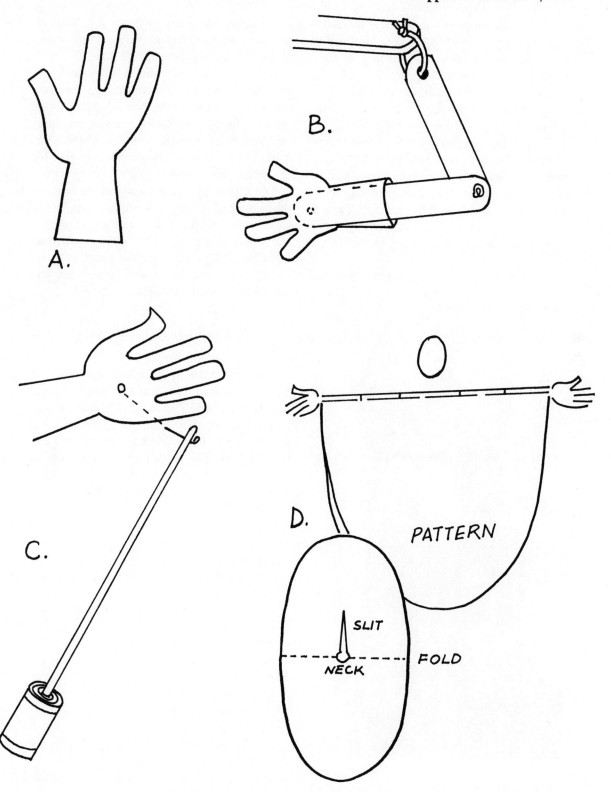

FIG. 8. Rod puppet patterns.

Explore the range of movement in the hand-and-rod puppet. Try holding the spine rod in your left hand, the two arm rods in your right hand. Reverse manipulating positions of your hands to see which feels more comfortable.

In the true rod puppet, the hand that holds the center body rod can also hold one of the arm rods. The puppeteer's other hand is free to manipulate one arm rod for specific gestures. The hand-and-rod puppet does not allow this shifting, so one must learn to manage both with one hand. A dangling arm rod (at eye level) can be a hazard to you and to other puppeteers working with you. Learn to manage the controls.

Gestures with rod puppets may be slow and

El Filósofo (The Philosopher), used in adult shows. Hand-and-rod puppet with plastic wood head created by Rafael Ruiz, Títeres de Borinquen, Puerto Rico.

sustained or sharp and vigorous. See what effect the draped garment suggests for movement. Could the puppet handle a cape?

Return to the exercises in Chapter VI to put the hand-and-rod figure through the same rehearsal process as the hand puppet. Enjoy the new discoveries of elbow action, sweeping reaches in the air, arms extending to the back. What hand and face relationships are possible in moving this puppet?

Could your puppet put one arm around another puppet? Could two puppets link arms? Could one puppet fold its arms across its waist? Could it pantomime holding and rocking a baby? Could this puppet enact a "mad" scene? Improvise to discover everything you can about the way it works.

THE STRING PUPPET (MARIONETTE) (See Fig. 9)

The marionette appeals to many beginners because the assembled figure suggests a miniature human (A). The marionette can be constructed of wood, plastic wood, Celastic, papier mâché, foam rubber, cloth, or any combination. The cloth marionette is easy to construct. The jointing is silent, and the figure responds well at the end of the strings.

Step 1.

Tools:
    sewing machine.
    scissors.
    sewing needle.
    straight pins.
    stuffing stick (½″ dowel, rounded end).
    ball-point pen.
    hammer and/or pliers.
    tin snips or heavy-duty shears.
Materials:
    unbleached muslin.
    #50 sewing thread.
    rigid cardboard.
    stuffing material (filler cotton, kapok, or dacron filler).
    sheet lead (plumbing supply, or lead fishing sinkers, or dress weights).
    pattern paper.

Peter from Peter and the Wolf *and Producer Peter Zapletan. The Children's Television Theatre, Mississippi Authority for Educational Television, 1972. Puppet design and construction by Jarmila and Peter Zapletal.*

Elmer's glue.

¾" masking tape.

Step 2. Draw figure to scale on brown paper or newsprint. A 24" marionette, representing a 6' adult, is a convenient size for the experiment. Scale 4" = 1'. The rough is primarily for size and proportions. Arms and legs will be basic tubes of material, so do not worry about drawing shapely limbs.

Step 3: Patterns and Adjustments. Study Figure 9A of the completed marionette. The joints (shaded areas) have no stuffing. Lead weights (black areas) assist gravity in those parts that rise and fall. Compare each part of the body with the pattern for it (B1 through B11). Arms, legs, and neck have *length added* to pattern. The extra material becomes a fabric tab for sewing each part to the body. Mark each pattern piece, as you make it, with notation to leave seam open for stuffing; or no

seam required (to make tab). Fold patterns at joints to divide the stuffed areas from the empty ones.

Head and *Body* shapes (full front view) are no problem.

Neck (stuffed portion) runs from body to point above middle of head at back. Add 2" to pattern length—1" for each tab top and bottom.

Arm, add 1" to top of designed length. Allow at least ½" for elbow joint, 1" for shoulder joint.

Hand is a simple mitt outline showing grouped fingers and separate thumb.

Leg is a semicircular stuffed tube, with a stop at knee joint so leg will bend in only one direction. It is put together with five easy pieces. The back of the leg is one continuous strip. The front of the leg is in two pieces (upper and lower) separated by ⅛" space. Two

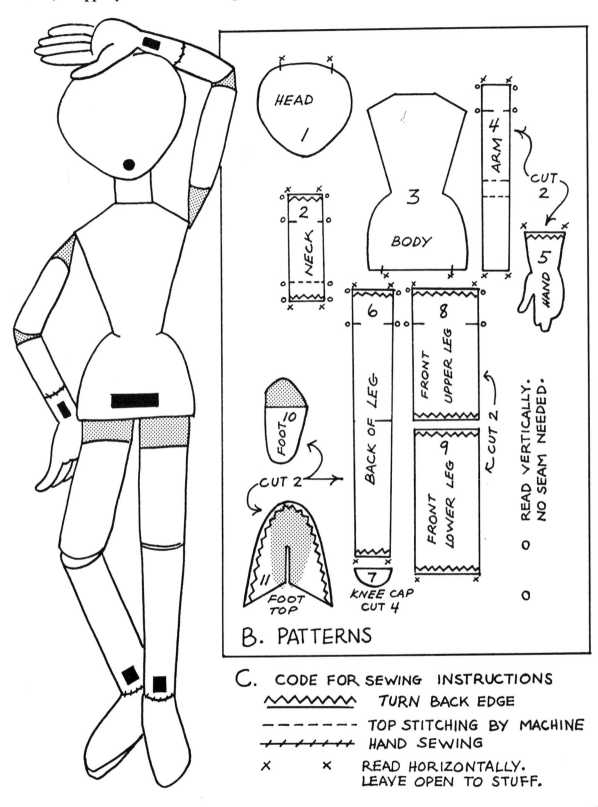

FIG. 9. *Construction of a marionette.*

kneecaps separate upper and lower leg, act as the stop, and keep the stuffing from falling out. Back pattern is your designed width. Kneecap is as wide as back of leg, with half-circle in front (B7). The distance around arc of kneecap is width of pattern for front of leg. Add 1″ to top of back pattern; add 1″ to upper front pattern.

Foot (2 pieces). A straight line runs across the ball of the foot (B10). Shaded area bends up (in construction) to create "rocker" action between sole of foot and toes for better puppet walking. Enlarge upper pattern as in B11. Straight edges join together at the back; curved section fits around foot.

Step 4: Cutting Instructions (fabric and cardboard). Position all pattern pieces on unbleached muslin (doubled). Spacing should include standard ½″ seam allowance for each piece. Trace patterns and cut. *Exceptions:* Use 1″ seam allowance for bottom pattern of foot (B10) and around the four kneecap pieces (B7).

Mark points on fabric where seams stop. Do not sew beyond.

Cut right and left foot (B10) from heavy cardboard. Score line across ball of foot, using heavy pressure of ball-point pen or light cut with knife. Cardboard bends with clean, straight edge along scored mark. Bend sections away from scoring.

Cut four kneecap pieces of heavy cardboard.

Fold back to pattern line all the edges marked 〜〜〜〜〜. Use thumbnail to crease these edges flat.

Step 5 (See Fig. 10): Machine Sewing (all parts except feet). Use large machine stitch (6 to 8 per inch). Short stitches tend to break as tension is applied to seams during stuffing.

Position front leg pieces (upper and lower) over back leg. Allow ⅛″-gap at knee. Match edges, and sew one side seam (10A). Match edges of other side, and sew seam (10B).

After sewing all pieces, clip seams at all points that dip inward: waist, hollow of thumb on hand, fingertip dips, and wrist. Turn back one seam edge; thumb-crease flat against

work. (Opened seams turn and stuff better.)

Turn pieces right side out, so all seams face inside.

Step 6: Top Stitching by Machine. After work has been turned right side out, machine stitching through both layers is a quick way to make some of the dividing lines.

Mark and top stitch the two divisions for elbow joint on arm (10C).

Mark and top stitch dividing lines for fingers on hand (10D).

Mark and top stitch base line for neck (10E).

Step 7: Hand Sewing

Kneecap. Use double thread to make a running stitch about ¼″ outside drawing on fabric. Place cardboard piece on muslin to match outline (F1). Pull thread to gather up fullness over the back side of the cardboard (like enclosing it in a tight-fitting sack, F2). Take a few stitches to anchor the gathering, then take lacing stitches across the work so cardboard cannot move inside casing. Hand sew a covered kneecap into each of the four leg openings. Smooth side faces out (F3).

Foot. Cut a piece of sheet lead in outline ¼″ smaller than cardboard foot. Use masking tape to bind lead to top of cardboard. Bend ball of foot up so tip is ⅜″ off level. (Lead liner will hold cardboard in position. See G).

Make a running stitch ¼″ outside foot outline on fabric. Pull thread, gather fullness of seam, anchor thread, and lace as for kneecap.

Thumb-crease seam edge for upper foot piece (H1). Pin front of upper to front of fabric edge on lower foot. Pin around to back and sew top to bottom (H2). Sew back seam. Slit on top is for stuffing.

Step 8: Prepare Lead Weights. The puppeteer must be able to feel the weight of the marionette to judge when the feet are firmly on the floor or when the seat is sitting in a chair. Weighting also adds momentum to the swing of the arm and the stance of the legs.

Sheet lead can be cut to any size with tin snips or heavy-duty kitchen shears. Cut a

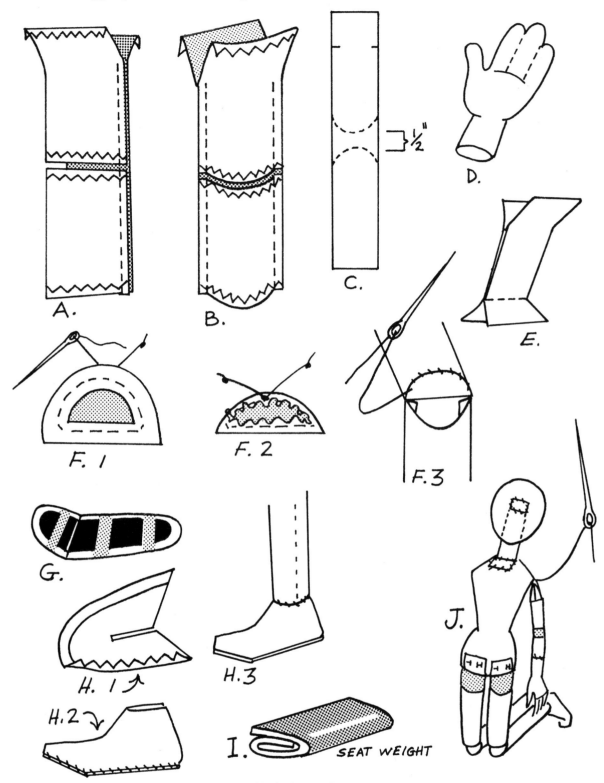

FIG. 10. Sewing marionette parts.

piece 3″ x 3″ for seat. Fold two sides over each other to make a triple thickness 1″ x 3″. Hammer flat or squeeze together with pliers (I). Make smaller weights for arms, legs, and chin. Lead weights are folded and wrapped with stuffing material before being inserted into body pieces, so that no blunt edges could wear through the fabric.

Step 9: Stuffing and Weighting. An old-time radio commercial claimed its product was "so round, so firm, so fully packed." The same words should apply to a good, stuffed cloth body. You will be surprised at how much stuffing the parts will hold if you keep adding to make firm, fully packed shapes.

Pack the head and body, using your fingers to push stuffing into place. Use a stuffing stick (½″ rounded dowel) for the longer tubes.

You can hand-shape and flatten work from outside as you go along. Don't pull against the seams, or they will pop.

Wrap lead weights with plenty of stuffing when you bury them so they cannot rub against fabric.

No stuffed portion should be floppy or squishy. With practice you can make a smooth shape without lumps.

Pinch fabric together, close to the stuffing, when hand sewing a section to seal off stuffing. Sew over and back for tight finish.

If thread breaks while sewing together bottom seam on body, use carpet thread, lace it together as far as it will go, and cut a piece of muslin to cover the gap. Hand sew muslin in place.

Fingers and Hand. When these individual finger "pockets" are stuffed, the effect will be rounded, separate fingers held together. At a distance, they are just as effective as a carved wooden hand. Stuff fingers and thumb first, then palm to wrist. No closure. Cuff fits over lower arm. You may need to use the blunt end of a crochet hook to pack stuffing in fingers.

Feet. Stuff through slit in top, being careful to retain angle bend at front of foot.

When stuffed, sew slit flaps over each other to make a flat surface for joining to ankle.

Neck. Top of the neck is the one exception, where stuffing could taper off to a flat point to make it easier to sew tab to head.

Step 10: Grand Assembly. Slip lower arm into cuff of hand, so that thumb is at right angles to the elbow joint. Pin cuffs in place. Allow a little play for wrist action. Sew hand cuff to arm.

Sew feet to legs.

Leg Top. Put pins across top joint line. Spread tabs and pin to front and back of body for both legs. Check balance. Both feet should touch floor at the same time. Adjust, if necessary. Remove legs, sew correct top line for leg joints. Repin legs in position (J) and sew tabs down permanently.

Arms. Pin in place to check length. Use only one layer of material; trim away other layer to reduce bulk of shoulder joint. Make running stitch at joint line of upper arm, pull it tight to shirr material into a point, knot thread, and sew point to tip of shoulder. Take enough stitches so arm will not pull loose during vigorous action.

Neck. Spread tabs front and back to center neck over seam line of body. Pin tabs in place, and sew all four sides of each tab to body.

Last step is to sew the tab (double thickness) at the top of the neck in position at the back of the head (J).

The jointed figure is now ready for action with the help of a few strings. Before moving on, try positioning the figure in various poses —kneeling, sitting, wide stance, cross-legged, etc. Holding the body by the waist, see if the legs will swing forward and back as the body is lifted up and down (one foot forward and one back, reversing positions on each lift). Move arms through full circle of movement.

Bug in a Rug, *original marionette production for the Cain Park Theatre, designed and directed by George Latshaw in 1946.*

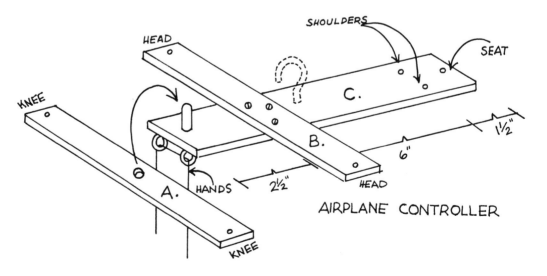

FIG. *11. Marionette controller.*

Check head action. I would prefer a marionette to be a little on the loose side and capable of broad actions, rather than stiff and restricted. A good figure can be handled with restraint; a poor one reaches its limits too soon.

CONTROLLER (See Fig. 11)

A wooden controller can be made of lattice, available at lumberyards in 1¼″ and 1½″ widths. The horizontal, airplane controller is popular in America, because it is easy to handle. The strings on it are spread apart enough to grasp easily. Dipping and tilting the "airplane" produces the head action.

Step 1.
Materials:
   1 strip lattice 1½″ x 10″ long for body bar (C).
   2 strips lattice 1¼″ x 8″ long for head bar (B) and leg bar (A).
   ½″-diameter wood dowel 1¼″ long—peg for foot bar.
   3 small wood screws and 2 small screw eyes (both with fine shank).
   white glue and sandpaper.
   1 cup hook, or large screw eye opened up to make hook.
Tools:
   coping saw or keyhole saw for cutting lattice.
   drill and bits for making holes.

Step 2: Cut, Drill, Sand and Join. Cut lattice pieces and wood dowel for controller to size.

Drill string holes at marked spots.

Drill hole for ½″ dowel peg 1″ back from front end of body bar (C).

Drill ⅝″ hole in center of foot bar (A). It must slip over dowel peg easily.

Sand all cut ends. Sand smooth all edges. Round off sharp corners. Round top of dowel peg, and sand.

Glue dowel peg in body bar. Center head bar 2½″ back from front of body bar. Glue and screw in place.

Place screw eyes in position on underside of body bar. The "eye" should face side view, so string can run through easily.

The cup hook or screw eye hook can be put in later, after figure has been strung. Find the balance point by resting controller on a fingertip. Footbar should be on peg. Hook is put in directly above the balance point.

STRINGING (See Fig. 12)

Many professionals use black, woven fish line (ranging from 5- to 20-lb. test, depending on the weight of the figure). If cost is a problem, you may substitute black carpet thread or button thread. It is less expensive and sturdy enough to support a cloth marionette. It does fray in time, and it is not as easy to untangle.

At each point where the string is to be attached to the body, take at least one full stitch through the material, and repeat, before tying the ends together. This will give the fastening a little more grip.

The length of the strings will depend on your elevation from the puppet stage floor. For a trial stringing, plan to work the marionette on the floor, with the controller held at waist level. Measure and cut two head strings and two shoulder strings, adding 6″ for tying off, which will span the distance between controller and marionette.

Sew and tie off strings on either side of head, just above the ears and just behind the center seam line (A1). Tie these off securely.

Sew and tie strings at top of each "shoulder blade" (A2). If they are placed directly on seam line, they will interfere with head movement. Shoulder strings should not rub against head when attached to controller.

Run head strings through holes in head bar. Tie each off in a slip knot after checking to make certain both controller and head are level. Insert right and left shoulder strings in controller. Adjust tension so that both are taut when controller is level. Tie a slip knot to hold in place. The figure is suspended and balanced between head and shoulder strings. By tipping controller forward, the puppet will bow its head. Hold that controller position; tilt head bar up on right side, and puppet will look right. Tilt left side of head bar up, and

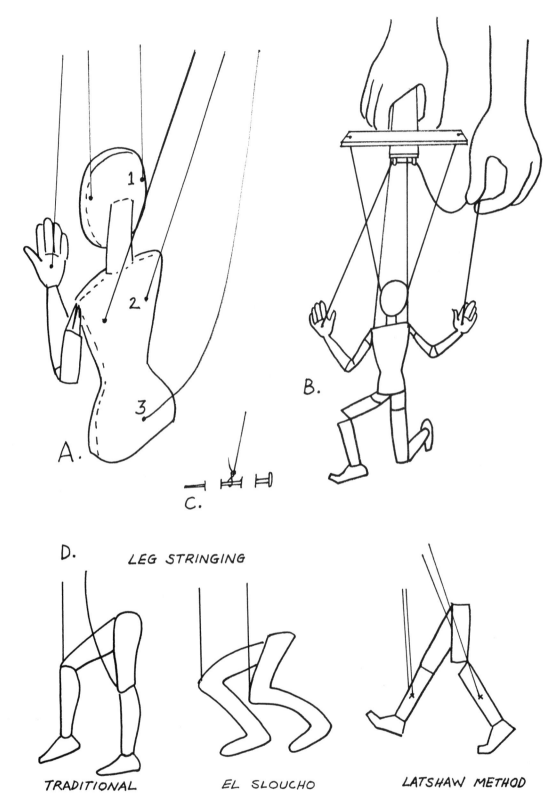

FIG. 12. *Stringing the marionette.*

head will turn in that direction. When these four strings are "set," they may be tied off with a series of knots.

The seat string is attached just where it says it is (A3). When controller is tipped forward, seat string should be almost taut. Tipping the controller should engage only the shoulder strings for head action. The seat string is pulled separately to make the puppet bow. When the controller is level, there is slack in the seat string.

Hand strings are tied to the palms of the hands. In this method the string runs from one hand up through the screw eyes in the controller and down to the other hand. The advantage to this is that either hand may be raised by pulling one string, or both may be raised if it is pulled far enough. To prevent arms from dangling lifelessly, tie off hand string just short of reaching the full length. One hand, slightly elevated, creates a more interesting pose when the figure is at ease, and

Jupiter, 44-inch marionette built by Don Sahlin for a proposed production of Rameau's opera Platee. *Note arm action.*

the pose is automatic because of the shorter stringing.

The continuous loop stringing between two points is also used with a hand-and-elbow, or hand-and-upper-arm combination, to extend the range of arm movements. Experiment: run a hand string up through one screw eye on controller and back down to the test point. Mark string and tie double knot there. Pin the knot to the body temporarily by stitching a straight pin through the material before and after running it through the knot at the point you want to join (12C). The knotted point stays securely in place for a tryout of action. The pinned knot can be moved easily to test other areas.

A convincing walk for the marionette is the bugaboo of puppeteers. Traditionally, the leg strings are tied to a point just above the knee. Strings run up to opposite ends of a detachable leg bar. As the bar is seesawed back and forth, the knees rise and fall. The body is moved forward at the same time the legs do their stiff march. If the body is not held erect during the walk, the marionette slinks into a Groucho Marx lope around the stage.

In 1950, while I was working on a marionette project for Burr Tillstrom, I devised an alternate method of stringing the legs, with these features:

Absence of ankle joint. Foot does not drop down when leg is raised.

Use of "rocker" action. Foot rolls forward from flat position onto the ball of the foot (which causes knee joint to bend open) before taking a step.

Addition of second string. The double-stringing puts the leg between two points of support in a sort of cradle, or sling, so that the movement can be balanced and guided more carefully.

Dropping of point of lift. Strings are attached at the sides of the "calf" in lower half of leg, well below the knee.

The two strings are tied off through a single hole in the leg bar, as in the other method, but they must be balanced more carefully so that each side pulls evenly. This unique stringing will also elevate the knee and move into a high kick. It is also excellent for helping the marionette move gracefully out of the position of being on both knees. Crossing the marionette's legs is no problem with this stringing. By holding the leg bar close to the controller, the feet can be lifted in such a way that the marionette can take backward steps. The limitation is that the stringing works best with a minimum of costume interference. Marionettes in pants, tights, opera hose, or short skirts benefit; the long-skirted and others will have to glide along as best they can.

Leg strings (either method) are long enough to permit the leg bar to be slipped over peg on main control without elevating the legs.

When all strings are in proper adjustment, tie them off at the controller in a series of knots. A dab of white glue on the knot will keep it from coming untied. Clip excess string ½″ from knot, so there are no dangling ends to tangle with manipulating strings.

To keep the marionette from tangling, tension should be kept on the strings by using it, or by hanging it. To pack it for storage, simply twirl figure so all strings form one strand (two or three turns is sufficient). Gather this strand close to controller, and wrap it round and round main controller (behind the head bar). Marionettes are stored in cloth bags with drawstring tops. The drawstring is tied around controller so the two elements will not separate. To unwrap, reverse the process. Untie the bag, pull out the marionette, gather the strand and unwrap, until figure can hang by twisted strand. Gently turn to unwind, and the marionette is ready to use again.

Untangling. The tangled marionette demonstrates the perversity of inanimate objects. The dropped foot bar or fallen controller demonstrates the carelessness of humans. Treat any mess as a puzzle to be unraveled a step at a time. Try to separate the foot bar and its strings first if possible. They can be laid on the floor out of the way, as you lift strings over the controller to put them back into their original positions.

JULIAN APSEL STUDIO PHOTO: VORIES FISHER

(Left) The Mayor *(right)* and Mistress of Hamelin from *The Pied Piper. Hand puppets by George Latshaw. Note the face design on this mayor and the one in the following photograph.* (Right) *A medieval Mayor and Lady, Bunraku-style puppets by George Latshaw for Martha Bennett King's original tale* The Story of UFO *(Miracle of Books Fair, Chicago, 1961). Note: Two "disguises" use the same makeup, but this puppet stands 4 feet tall. The Lady has a tripod under her skirt instead of legs, so she can stand alone.*

Manipulation. Prop a mirror on the floor at an angle that will give you the best view of your marionette. Discover what it will do. Have it walk, kneel, kick, jump, stride. Give it a box to sit on. Can it swing its legs; can it cross them? Can it lie on its back and look up at the stars? Can it breathe and sigh? Can it think? Can it feel emotion? What will the arms do? How will it speak?

The traditional puppeteers specialized in one type of figure, perfecting their technique with it over a lifetime. Contemporary puppeteers are more flexible in their approach, often trying a different puppet type for each production. Each encounter with a new or unfamiliar puppet is an adventure in training. The puppeteer who is able to learn from each experience builds a broader view of what it means to be an animator of objects.

The traditional puppet stage concealed the puppeteers, provided a frame for the action, and hid the secret workings from the public. The stage served as a moat to keep the real world at a distance, and as a fortress to guard the mystery of the diminutive beings who appeared there. Concealment was essential to preserve the illusion that the figures were independently alive.

Today there is a trend to liberate both puppets and puppeteers from the confines of the traditional stage masking. Puppeteers have come out of hiding to work in full view of the audience. They have invaded the stage space of the actor's theatre, and a few have even moved out of the building to perform in the streets. As a result the puppets have grown larger to capitalize on their new freedom in new environments. To trace the developments in contemporary staging, we shall begin with an X-ray view of traditional stages.

MARIONETTE STAGE (See Fig. 13)

The basic structure for a marionette stage consists of platforms on two levels that are connected to the frameworks used to suspend front masking, lights, backdrops, and marionettes.

The lower platform (A) serves as the stage floor for the marionettes. It is usually 12″ to 18″ high to raise the marionettes into a better line of vision for the audience. It does not have to be a weight-bearing structure unless the puppeteer must walk on it to change sets and props. The second, higher platform is called the bridge (B). It is the walkway on which the puppeteers stand 3 to 4 feet above the floor level. The bridge must be sturdy enough to support the weight of two or three puppeteers without creaking. Ladder(s) (C) are placed at sides or rear of bridge.

The largest framework (D) holds up the

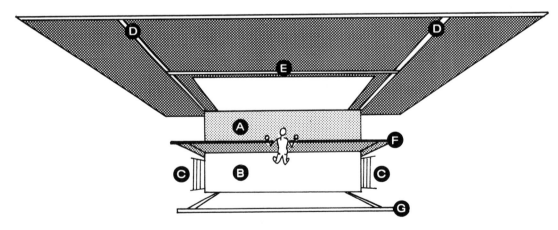

FIG. *13. Marionette stage line.*

102

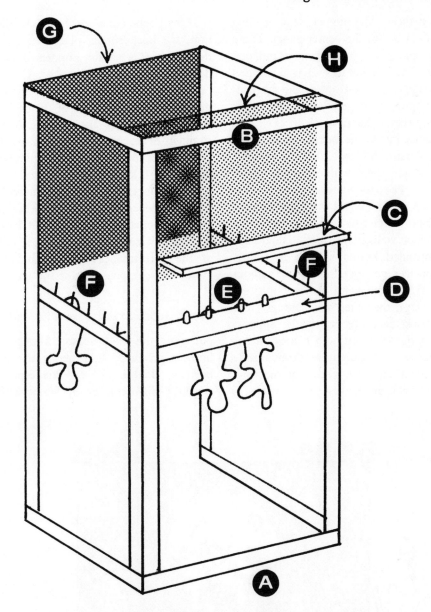

FIG. 14. Traditional "Punch and Judy" booth.

front masking drapery. The cross-bracing (E) also holds lights and act curtain above the proscenium opening. The second framework is called the backdrop rail or leaning rail (F), since it serves both functions. Puppeteers use the waist-high railing to brace themselves when they must reach far forward. Rolled backdrops, tied off at the leaning rail, can be released as required for fast scene changes. The third framework, running behind the bridge, is called the puppet rail (G), where offstage marionettes are hung while waiting for their cues.

ONE-PERSON HAND-PUPPET STAGE (See Fig. 14)

The traditional "Punch and Judy" booth is a three-sided, folding screen (A). The top and rear of the booth are also masked for outdoor performances. The puppet stage opening (B) runs the width of the center panel. There is no wing space, so puppets enter and exit from below. The playboard (C) is a wooden ledge running across the front of the stage. It serves as an apron, or stage floor, to hold props and scenic pieces. The prop shelf (D) is a tray suspended inside the booth, directly below the playboard. All items that the puppets handle are stored there within easy reach of the puppeteer. Pegs for hanging puppets may be located on a bar (E) at the back edge of the prop shelf, or on bars (F) running across the right and left walls of the booth. Hand puppets are suspended, bottom-side up, by a ring, so the puppeteer can get into them without assistance. While one hand of the puppeteer is busy on stage, the other hand plunges into a puppet backstage, lifts it off the support peg, turns it right-side up, and makes an entrance. After an exit, the puppet drops upside down, the hand slips out, grabs for the ring, and places it back on the peg.

If the puppeteer works in the overhead position, the backdrop is placed at the back of the booth (G) so the puppets move the full depth and width of the space. Contemporary puppeteers sacrifice stage depth by holding the puppets directly in front of themselves at eye level. The puppets are confined to a narrow channel of space (determined by the puppeteer's reach) between the playboard and the scrim backdrop (H). The scrim backdrop can be a single-knit jersey or any other fabric with the properties of a one-way mirror, allowing the puppeteer to see out but blocking the audience's view in. The puppeteer's clear view of the performance from behind the scrim more than compensates for the lack of depth.

MULTIMEDIA STAGE (See Fig. 15)

During the 1948 season Martin and Olga Stevens produced and performed a double-barreled double bill by Shakespeare. They staged *The Taming of the Shrew* with rollick-

FIG. *15. Multimedia stage.*

ing, robust hand puppets. They used somber, stately rod puppets to portray the tragic characters of *Macbeth*. The Three Witches appeared as eerie shadows silhouetted against the sky. During the show of Kings, each image appeared sharply in glowing, stained-glass colors, then seemed to blur, expand, and vanish in the mist. Their perfect casting matched each type of puppet to the role it could do best, and mixed them on a stage that they could use together.

Hand, rod, and shadow puppets all could be operated from below, and the two puppeteers sat on rolling stools so that the figures would appear at the most favorable sight line for the audience. The playing area (A) resembled a thrust stage extending from the playboard (B) back to the unit set (C), which formed the back wall. There was no proscenium. Entrances were provided through the arched doorways (D) upstage right and left, with a suggestion of the battlements above. The upstage center area contained a screen (E), which remained plain for *Shrew* but was lit from behind to form the shadows for *Macbeth*. The functional simplicity of the unit set could accommodate Shakespeare's changing locales for both productions.

DESIGNING THE STAGE

Puppet stages are designed to meet the needs of the puppet, the puppeteer, and the production. There is no plan for a "one size fits all" stage that would meet the needs of every person reading this book, whereas, by defining your own needs, you can design your own unique stage.

Your need for *mobility* determines the *space*.
Your need for *space* determines *dimensions*.
Your need for *concealment* determines the *structures/materials*.
Your need for *portability* determines the *units*, etc., etc.

Continue the list with performance needs of your own.

Now, consider the ventriloquist working with a dummy (i.e., a large, jointed doll articulated by one person who speaks for it.) Then consider the Bunraku theatre, also working with a large, jointed doll, but articulated by three persons and requiring a fourth person to

Steve Hansen's walking street theatre for Punch and Judy is alive with action. Hansen's slogan is, "If the show fits, wear it!"

"The Story Wagon" is a unique covered-wagon hand-puppet stage for both indoor and outdoor performances. Ruthmarie, the storyteller, sits out front holding Grannie Annie Maria, a lap puppet. They interact with puppets on stage and occasionally play roles in the plays with the puppets. Puppeteer Betty Polus is behind the scenes doing all the puppet roles. Onstage, in this view, are Anna Maria Andersen and Hans Christian Andersen, as a young boy, to introduce "The Tinderbox and Other Tales."

speak for it. Similar puppets, but different needs on the part of the performers, the puppets, and the production. The Japanese have different needs for mobility, stage space, concealment, vocal assistance, and stylized movement in the full figure. The ventriloquist eliminates the need for a stage; the Bunraku performers capitalize on the use of human theatre space. The Bunraku puppeteer whose manipulation achieves perfection is given the name of a distinguished predecessor and excused from wearing the black costume and hood. The artistry of these honored ones transcends the need for concealment.

For those who expressed a need for "measurements" on the list above, we can play a

Bunraku puppet drama dates back to the 16th century and achieved its present form in the 18th century. It is performed regularly at the Bunraku-za Theatre in Osaka. The elaborate, half-life-size dolls and their manipulators appear on a full-scale theatre stage.

game of "Design-a-Stage" to develop a model for string puppets.

PHASE I (See Fig. 15).

All measurements are to be given in feet or simple fractions of feet (¼, ½, etc.). If you prefer, go metric, using meters and decimeters. Where your own measurements are required, use tape measure, yardstick, or metric ruler so that your size is recorded accurately. If no guideline is given, put down your best estimate for other measurements. These can be tested later.

As you complete the questionnaire enter your figures in the numbered blanks below.

1)____ height of marionette platform (between 1' and 2', or?).
2)____ height of marionette.
3)____ height of space you need above figure to give it good framing. Stage openings are sometimes based on a ratio of 1½, 2, 2½, etc. times the height of the figure. Or be arbitrary. Enter real measurement in the space, not ratio.
4)____ Add #2 and #3 = height of proscenium opening.
5)____ Additional height needed above proscenium opening to mask audience sight lines into working area.
6)____ Your height from floor to waist (or higher). The spot you pick should be comfortable for bracing against leaning rail.
7)____ Your height from point #6 to the top of your head (6 + 7 = your total height; if it does not, measure again).
8)____ Height above your head needed for masking.
9)____ Add #'s 1, 2, 3, 5, 7, and 8. Enter the height from stage floor to top of your marionette stage masking.
10)____ Add #'s 1, 4, and 5. Enter total, the height from floor to top of backdrop rail.

11)____ Subtract #6 from #10. Enter that number, the height of the puppeteer's bridge from floor level.

PHASE 2 (See Fig. 16).

Enter your measurements and estimates on depth in the numbered blanks below.

1)____ Length of your arms held out in front of you. Can you increase this distance by bending forward without moving your feet? What depth do you need for your marionette stage?

2)____ Lay yardstick or metric rule on floor. Determine the depth of bridge by space you need to stand on. Would you feel secure on a bridge 2' deep, or 6 decimeters deep? Could you get by with less? Do you need more? (Refer to #11 in Phase I—this is the bridge height off the floor.)

3)____ How far can you reach from the bridge back to the puppet rail? How much distance do puppets need to

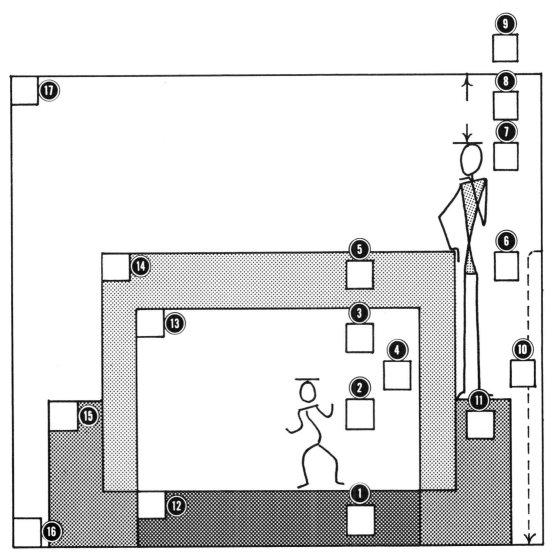

FIG. 15. *Design-a-Stage Game—front view.*

hang free, without bumping into bridge platform?

4)____ Add #'s 1, 2, and 3. Enter total, the depth of your setup on stage.

PHASE 3

Estimate the widths for each section below, and enter in numbered blanks below.

12)____ Width of puppet stage floor. (Does it stop at proscenium line, or could it have hinged extensions?)

13)____ Width of proscenium. What would make a pleasing rectangle?

14)____ Width of backdrop rail. How much "extra" do you need to mask sight-lines into the wings? Could the off-stage part of the rail be an extension arm, angled downstage to block the view, without cutting down space for entrances?

15)____ Width of bridge. Would it have to be as long as it appears in the illustration? Could it be less wide than the backdrop rail?

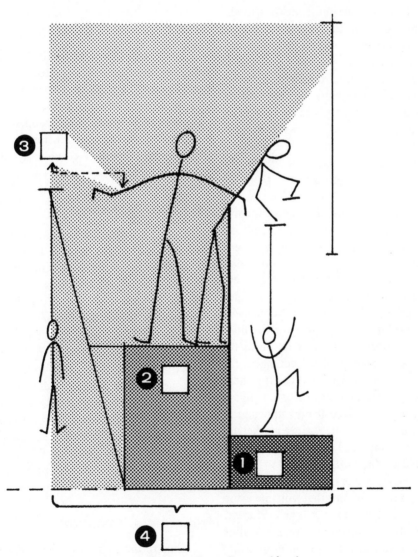

FIG. 16. Design-a-Stage Game—side view.

16)＿＿ How much width do you need beyond proscenium opening? Figure for one side (1', 2', 3', or?) Since you must figure the extension for both sides of proscenium, double the number for a single side, and enter it.

17)＿＿ Add #'s 13 and 16 = total width of stage setup with masking. Does this make a pleasing rectangle with the established height of the setup?

PHASE 4

To really understand what all these written measurements mean, one must make a model to scale. The model in the diagram could not change to accommodate the varied measurements transferred there, so it is necessary to see your estimate in three dimensions. Select an inch scale or centimeter scale that will result in a model of adequate size to view carefully from all sides. It is not necessary to construct the model for any structural considerations at this time. It is simple to check the relationships of measurements for their effectiveness.

From a sheet of construction paper or cardboard, cut a piece to represent the height and width of masking. Cut out proscenium opening. Form two boxes to represent puppet platform and puppeteers' bridge. Cut one piece to represent backdrop area, and tape or glue it at appropriate height to the puppeteer's bridge. Cut a solid piece of paper for the floor to puppet rail distance. Tape it in place for the appropriate angle. Cut a rectangle, the scale height of your marionette. Fold it in half, so it will stand up, and draw a stick figure string puppet on it. Place it on puppet platform. Cut another rectangle your scale height. Fold in half to stand up. Draw yourself on one surface. Stand on the bridge.

You now have a working model to study and ponder. You may feel that you have too much of this, and too little of that. Phase 5 would allow for revision, and in succeeding phases there would be the translation into materials, the breakdown into portable units, the

actual construction, and the final testing in transportation and performance.

When you have finished these phases, you may decide you need (a) a loan from the bank for a larger vehicle; (b) a much simpler stage, perhaps with no front masking; or (c) to work on the floor with no stage at all. You might even decide to shift to another type of puppet and start the "Design-a-Stage" game all over again.

Today's puppeteers will not be pinned down to merely perpetuating the past. There have been too many influences pushing them into the future.

THE END OF ANONYMITY

The puppeteers of the 1920's and 1930's did not inherit the family "secrets." They were self-taught. They had to carve their own names in puppetry, to create their own identities through their work. They dropped the masking without dropping the illusion. The audience moved up a notch from naive to knowing the persons behind the scenes.

GOODBYE PROSCENIUM

Burr Tillstrom jumped into television, proscenium and all, to become an instant hit with *Kukla, Fran and Ollie.* Canadian puppeteer John Conway and television producer-director Norm Campbell pioneered in the use of the camera to frame the puppets on *The Uncle Chichimus Show* for CBC Toronto. This inventive team was in the avant garde discovering the new mobility, the inventive mix with live actors, the sliding scale of puppet environments, the new freedom that only the camera could provide. Their work was a landmark for all that followed. Live audiences expected puppets to continue the same imaginative approaches to staging that they had seen on their home screens.

SEARCH FOR TOMORROW

Theatre the world over is searching for new ways of relating to audiences by theatre-in-the-

COURTESY YAKIMA HERALD

The rocketlike thrust to hand-puppet stage design by George Latshaw was inspired by reading about Raymond Loewy's work in industrial design. Cardboard model rests atop the playboard for inspection by Cookie Crocodile and Latshaw. George Walton (left) constructed the test model from fiber board (1953).

PHOTO: JOE BODNAR

Rocket stage design translated into prototype of slender aluminum tubing, taut canvas, and wood by Austin Cox of the industrial design firm of Smith, Scherr & McDermott. This backstage view shows lightboard fitted into compact playboard-prop shelf unit. Special fittings were manufactured to join the various angles of the thrust construction.

PHOTO: JOE BODNAR

Stage dimensions were tailored to the height of the puppeteer, so that projecting arms for the lights could be attached from floor level.

PHOTO: JOE BODNAR

Backstage view. The width of the stage was geared to the reach of the puppeteer. Puppets were hung from the back ledge of the prop shelf. Visible through the scrim backdrop are onstage characters from The Pied Piper.

The television camera was much more flexible than the fixed proscenium in "framing" what the audience could see. Natalie Hackenschmidt, a visitor from the States, was met with antique car by Canadian host, Uncle Chichimus.

Out of camera range, the innovative Canadian puppeteer John Conway talks with American guest puppeteer George Latshaw.

round, thrust staging, environmental theatre, happenings, theatre in the streets. Puppeteers have experimented with all forms, and many have introduced Western audiences to the Japanese Bunraku manner of staging with contemporary works for Western audiences. From the streets to symphony halls to cathedrals, puppets have been exploring new environments to find their own new audiences.

SEARCH FOR STATUS

There seems to be a world trend on the part of puppeteers to move their disguises into the actors' world of living theatre. There are those who fear it will weaken the strain of "pure" puppetry, but that will not deter those who are ready to pit wits. Puppeteers have been looked down on by theatre folk for too long to miss this chance to bid for equal rights. Anyone who has watched Edgar Bergen, Burr Tillstrom, Shari Lewis, Bruce Schwartz, or Jim Henson at work will have no trouble separating the stars from the straight characters. When it comes to puppets and people stealing stage, the puppets are no dummies.

PHOTO: LEONARD SCHUGAR

Bunraku Mime, Marionette Theater Arts Council; Margo Lovelace, lead puppeteer.

PHOTO: GARY BOYNTON

Freedom: A Patchwork of Progress, *Bicentennial program with the Lansing Symphony, produced by Pemrad Puppets with a grant from the Michigan Council for the Arts. The production included shadows, black theater manipulation, two dancers, and two narrators to Aaron Copland's* Music for the Theatre. *Directed by George Latshaw.*

Chapter XI

PUPPET PLAYS AND PLAYWRITING

Puppeteers searching for suitable scripts will be relieved to know that the repertoire does not begin and end with "Punch and Judy." The range of puppet plays is as varied as the tastes and personalities of the puppeteers themselves. These are some of the sources that have been tapped for puppets:

The published puppet play (see Bibliography)
Plays from the human theatre
Dramatizations from literature
Reader's theatre staging of a literary work
Revue sketches, skits, and blackouts
Original scripts
Solo or group improvisation on a theme
Scenarios of silence—mimed to symphonic music
Operas on records staged with puppets
Mixed media—human actors and puppets

The first professionals to share their plays in print were Tony Sarg, Catherine Reighard, Remo Bufano, and Edith Flack Ackley. Forman Brown's witty pieces for the Yale Puppeteers were brought out as a collection. The most recent published playwrights are Tom Tichenor, Eleanor Boylan, Lewis Mahlman, and David Jones. Bernard Shaw wrote a short play, *Shakes vs. Shav,* for his friends Muriel and Waldo Lanchester to perform with their marionettes in England. Some scenes from the Japanese doll theatre repertory are available in translation, and almost every how-to book on puppetry includes at least one sample script. All are worth reading for the insights they offer on writing for puppets.

Gordon Craig's vision of a more serious use of the marionette inspired some puppeteers to use the classics of the human theatre. Plays by Aristophanes, Euripides, Shakespeare, Molière, Rostand, Ibsen, O'Neill, and Gertrude Stein have had their hour on the puppet stage. Those productions stretched the dimensions of the puppet theatre by appealing to an adult audience. The puppet is not often asked to play the noble and heroic roles.

As in children's theatre, many puppeteers produce plays derived from literature. There is security in working with material that is both familiar and successful. Puppeteers find it less trouble to sell a production with a title that does not have to be explained. Scripts run from faithful interpretations of the original work to flights of fancy on the title theme. A "dramatization" attempts to render the original work faithfully in dramatic form. An "adaptation" may take liberties by rearranging scenes and judiciously pruning extraneous characters and events. A play "based on" a story means anything the rewrite person can get by with. Character names and major events are retained, but the treatment may give the material such a new slant as to make it an outright satire or a camp version of the original.

These are a few of the authors whose stories have inspired puppeteers:

Aesop
Hans Christian Andersen
L. Frank Baum
Lewis Carroll
Carlo Collodi
Charles Dickens

114

Lady Macbeth, a character in "Excerpts from Shakespeare" produced by the National Theatre of Puppet Arts.

The Old Man Faust from Fantasy on Faust, *designed and created by Daniel Llords for Llords' "International."*

Backstage (left to right), Old Man, Cassandra, and Herald, *9-foot puppets for Agamemnon. Produced at the University of Oklahoma in 1966, it was directed by Nat Eek; costume design was by Nancy Gade, and puppet design and construction were by George Latshaw.*

Aurora Valentinetti, of the Department of Drama, University of Washington, was commissioned by the Dean and Vestry to design and direct a production of Everyman *in the chancel of St. Mark's Cathedral, Seattle. Miss Valentinetti, shown here with Everyman, designed the fourteen characters as Javanese-style rod puppets; the 5-foot figures required two manipulators each.*

The Taming of the Shrew *(a cut version), showing Katharina, Grumio, Petrucchio, and Shakespeare. The "author" (W. S.) was pressed into playing minor roles: Kate's father, the tailor, and—even the horse! Hand puppets by Martin and Olga Stevens, 1948.*

The Taming of the Shrew *(unspoken Shakespeare) as a mime for two hands (His and Hers) to music from* Hand in Glove, *George Latshaw Puppets, 1958. Above: Kate shows her temper after Petrucchio has found the food unfit.*

A happy ending for The Shrew *as Kate and mate express approval of each other. George Latshaw Puppets.*

Washington Irving
Rudyard Kipling
A. A. Milne
Edgar Allan Poe
Robert Louis Stevenson
James Thurber
Mark Twain
Oscar Wilde

The allegories, myths, legends, parables, fantasies, and fables of other lands also offer a rich resource to those who are seeking ideas.

A word of caution: Do not "borrow" anything you find in print unless you ask permission *first!* Published material is protected under the copyright laws, which restrict its use, in any form, without express permission from the author or publisher. It does not matter whether your purpose is educational, charitable, or commercial; the only courteous and legal way to proceed is to obtain the right before making a dramatization or adaptation of any writing by another author. Permission may be denied, of course, or it may be granted on a limited basis for restricted use, or under the terms of a royalty agreement. Do not assume that a dead author's work is up for grabs, for the author's estate or heirs may continue to control the rights. Check first to save any legal embarrassment that might arise from an "innocent" but unauthorized production.

A playwright is like a blind prophet, who searches mentally for the sights and sounds of a future event. It is lonely and lengthy work. Many others must work with the vision before the playwright's "sight" is restored by seeing the prophecy played out upon the stage.

There is a maxim that plays are not written, but rewritten. Anyone who has tried to write a play will agree, for it requires more levels of imagination simultaneously than most of us can manage. Each draft reveals some flaw that was overlooked the time before. It is annoying that the perfect play does not flow through the typewriter or ball-point pen the first time around, or the second time, or the third, etc. Persons who understand the creative process are prepared for relentless pursuit. It is in the merry chase that one bumps into those unexpected combinations of ideas that shape a play in its final form.

Playwriting is a paper improvisation, requiring more paper (expense), and more patience (time) for each replay (revision). A more direct method for most of us is to turn playwriting from a mental process into a physical and vocal one of spontaneous improvisation. By working things out "live" we can see and hear as we go along, building a step at a time, letting one idea suggest another, until the shape of the play begins to emerge. It is swift, it is physical, and it is fun. What we throw out will not fill up a wastebasket, and what we decide to keep can be stored in our heads until we feel like putting it down on paper.

Where to start? An idea? A set of characters? A story? A locale? A theme? Any single one will do for a beginning if you are enthusiastic about it. All the elements will come into play sooner or later during the process of developing the improvisation into a play. Each element of a play requires us to answer questions that will enlarge our understanding of the material and contribute to the wholeness of the work. What puppets do on stage can be as important as what they say. As we check each element the possibilities for business, movement, action, and drama should be examined. We are staging the play as we go along.

The Theme is a succinct statement of what the play is about. Examples:

A fool and his money are soon parted.
She who laughs last, laughs best.
A man convinced against his will is of the same opinion still.

The theme does not have to be stated directly in the play, but it should be evident to the audience if they were asked to give a one-sentence summary.

The Form is the type of drama that would suit the theme, plot, or characters you wish to use. Form gives direction and style to the treatment of the material. Fantasy, farce, comedy, satire, melodrama, tragedy, epic, Grand

PHOTO: LARRY ENGLER

Aesop's Fables, *by the Poko Puppets.*

COURTESY PETER ZAPLETAL

The Steadfast Tin Soldier, *produced in 1976 by Peter Zapletal for the Mississippi Authority for Educational Television.*

The Tinderbox, *by the Coad Canada Puppets with a script by Victor Hay. The sleeping Princess is carried on the back of one of the immense-eyed magic dogs.*

The Scarecrow from Oz, by the Stevens Puppets.

PHOTO: PETER VOINESCU

The Hunter and the Wolf from Little Red Riding Hood, *by Eugene and Galina Naum.*

PHOTO: ARTHUR W. TONG

Ananse the Spider. *The Puppet Playhouse of New Orleans commissioned playwright Charles Kerbs to adapt the Ananse trickster tales from Ghana for this production. Ray J. Poret played the village storyteller as liaison between the rod-puppet animals and the audience.*

Guignol (grotesque horror), and science fiction are forms used in writing.

The Plot is the main story line or plan of action for a play. The plot tells us where the story begins, where it ends, and what happens in between. Although this sounds incredibly simple, many a play has floundered because it had no satisfactory ending. It may start well enough, continue agreeably, and then die, as if the author has given up rather than bringing the story to a strong conclusion. The playwright must be able to forecast the ending of the play from the outset and should consciously lead the audience to anticipate the climax scene from the moment the play starts. No one should have to ask, "Is it over now?" The plot will identify the central character, state that character's goals, introduce us to the opposing characters and events that will stand in the way and stir things up with enough conflict to cause a confrontation, a victory over the opposition, and a quick conclusion or denouement.

Characters and Locales can be starting points for story building. Movie sequels and television serials use this method to extend the adventures of a known group of characters. *M.A.S.H., Star Trek, Mary Tyler Moore, Maud,* and other series win us over with characters that make us wonder what will happen next time. You can start with a favorite puppet or one you can invent. Move it into a plot situation by asking the question, "What would happen if—?"

IF Mr. Punch decided to run for President?
IF Mr. Punch made contact with UFO's?
IF Mr. Punch landed James Bond's role as 007?

Mr. Punch would meet each situation in his characteristically outrageous way. As characters are tested in different situations, they begin to grow on us. We understand them better, because they remain consistent wherever they are, whatever they do. Another character facing the same situations would react differently and lead us to new situations. Cast Judy (Punch's wife), or Maud, or Bob Hope, or Woody Allen in any of the above "iffy" situations and imagine the changes the story lines would take.

Some writers start with the "where" of a story by picking an exotic locale. They pursue the rest by asking the journalist's questions of "who," "what," "when" and "how" to discover what took place there and to whom. What strikes your fancy as an exotic locale? Pick a place and track down a story there.

A curious café in the Casbah?
A wax museum after closing time?

Once you have decided on theme, plot, characters, and locale, you can start to improvise, taking time to develop each segment thoroughly before moving on to the next. Structure meaningful action into the puppet play. Work out your first improvisations without words. As you do a segment, ask these questions:

1) Where and when does this scene take place?
2) Who is in it?
3) What happens?
4) How does this scene move the story forward?
5) What is the objective of this scene?

How much of this information could you put across without speaking?

Improvisation #1
Play through the scene in pantomime. Is it possible? Is there anything for the puppets to *do* in the scene?

Improvisation #2
Repeat the same scene, adding vocal sounds but no words, to discover what the characters are feeling about themselves, about each other, about the situation they are in. Use sighs, yawns, humming, grrrs, teeth chattering, gulps, sniffs, giggles, hisses, cheers, gasps, screams,

moans, groans, guffaws, etc. Does the improvisation with basic sounds and movement make the scene clearer and more dramatic? Nontheatre people tend to avoid any emotional display in public. When this social custom is carried into the puppet show, the result is "staged storytelling" rather than a real play. Emotion is essential to drama, so we must structure the feelings for each character.

Improvisation #3

Improvising with dialogue should be the last step. Exhaust all other means of communication before using speech, and then use it sparingly. Beginning puppeteers tend to overuse dialogue to describe and explain everything until all feeling is washed away in a sea of talk. Dialogue should reveal the differences in the way each character thinks, feels, and speaks. It may be necessary to improvise dialogue many times to discover the right lines for each character. Actors are able to sustain long speeches much better than puppets, so it is wise to be brief. Revising, editing, and polishing dialogue can pare it down to the essence. Dialogue improvisation is not completed until actors are able to act it, the director is able to stage it, and the audience is able to believe it.

COMMITMENT TO MATERIAL

One of the essential ingredients for successful playwriting (or improvisation) is an enthusiastic commitment to the material. With this attitude, one is inspired to give the best effort to the project. If you do not care for an idea and have no respect for it, drop it and move on to something else you can work on with conviction. There are times when a puppeteer may be tempted to write for the market, a play about history, the Bicentennial, ecology, or whatever theme "sells" at the time. This can be a terrible trap, with disappointing results for both playwright and audience. Un-

COURTESY NATIONAL BROADCASTING COMPANY, INC.

A scene from Quillow and the Giant, *the NBC Children's Theatre musical-drama version of James Thurber's* The Great Quillow. *The musical score was by Ralph Blane (of* Meet Me in St. Louis) *and Wade Barnes. Quillow (George Latshaw) stands in a tower to talk to the Giant Hunder (Win Stracke). The show was produced and directed by David Barnhizer in 1963.*

less your interest in the material is genuine, avoid it, or the results will seem contrived and phony.

Criteria for playwriting should include questions on the special contributions of the puppets. Is the idea suitable for puppets? Can they perform it better than live actors? What special perspective or new knowledge will the audience gain from seeing the play done with puppets?

Puppet imagery can help us see other worlds in other ways. Suppose the theme were to deal with the problems of aging. Instead of using an old man and old woman (puppets) in a retirement center scene, we choose a discarded pop can and a spotted mirror with a cracked frame as our two characters, and shift the setting to the town dump. There the two have landed because they are old and of no use to anyone. They might act out their better days for us, and even plot ways to be discovered and rescued so they could go on being useful to someone.

The combination of live actors with puppets has endless possibilities. Is there any better way to stage *Pinocchio,* for instance, than to combine the flesh-and-blood Geppetto with a real, wooden marionette on strings?

The combination worked well in *To Dream a Dinosaur.* A young lad hatched a baby dinosaur (a 22″ hand puppet). In a short time, the dinosaur had grown to 7 feet tall (actor manipulating inside costume of dinosaur), and by the final scene the dinosaur had grown to 16 feet tall (a supersized rod puppet requiring four manipulators). This final version appeared during a night scene as a giant-sized outline cartoon to emphasize that the illusion had grown to preposterous proportions. In the climax scene, when the boy owner decided to give up the dinosaur, we were able to make it vanish and melt under black light. The dinosaur head vanished instantly, and the body outlines slowly drifted in a downward jumble as the dream collapsed. Using the puppet allowed

PHOTO: HASTINGS-WILLINGER & ASSOCIATES

Pinocchio, *adaptation by George Latshaw for a 1958 Cain Park Theatre production. Here Pinocchio tries to escape from the clutches of The Fire Eater.*

PHOTO: WES MOREFIELD

To Dream a Dinosaur, *produced by George Latshaw for the Summer Repertory season of the University of Oklahoma in 1971. The surprised boy hatches a dinosaur from an egg that he has kept hidden under his windbreaker.*

PHOTO: WES MOREFIELD

Mother is doubtful about a dinosaur as a family pet.

PHOTO: WES MOREFIELD

The dinosaur shoots up overnight to stand 7 feet tall. Here, the housekeeper is about to be surprised by the size of the family pet.

PHOTO: WES MOREFIELD

The 16-foot "Nightmare" dinosaur in the final scene was painted with fluorescent color. Under black light, the black figures of the puppeteers were invisible.

the dinosaur to grow from a funny baby animal to an overwhelming mysterious force to confront the human actors.

Peggy Wood, the noted actress, has described the 3 E's of theatre in this way:

To Entertain—To Educate—To Exalt

We are frequently entertained in the theatre, sometimes educated through the playwright's insight, and on rare occasions we may be exalted. A playwright should strive to achieve all three, for what else can match the exhilaration of being in the presence of excellence in the performing arts?

The theatre director is the major decision-maker for a production and the person responsible for guiding it from start to stage. The director sets the interpretation of the script, then channels the work of designers, actors, and technicians toward the fullest realization of that interpretation. The unity and style of the production depend on the director's ability to instruct, influence, and inspire many co-workers toward a common vision. Solo puppeteers sometimes concede that the director is the "missing link" in their productions.

The dilemma occurs naturally. During the early planning stages it is possible for the soloist to function in several capacities: selecting the script, setting the interpretation, and even shaping the design elements and their execution. In rehearsal the puppeteer steps out of the director's role by stepping into the performer's role. Some soloists try to solve the problem by rehearsing in front of a mirror. It is not difficult to approximate the audience view of hand puppets or marionettes in this way, but a rehearsal is more than a visual exercise, and other production elements cannot be monitored in a mirror. The puppeteer ceases to be an objective overseer of the whole while functioning as one of the parts. The lack of a director may be justified for reasons of economy or ego. In one case, it is a salary saved; in the other, it preserves the "artistic unity" of the soloist. Even if a puppeteer does not wish to surrender authority to a "guest director," another pair of eyes and ears is needed to provide honest feedback. A "coach" might be a less threatening term for a person who could advise the soloist in a calm, supportive manner during the rehearsal process of building a performance. It is much better to seek help than to try to rehearse in a vacuum.

The need for a director is obvious if a production requires two or more puppeteers. Rehearsals follow the same pattern used in live theatre, except that there are special considerations for the training, traffic patterns, and physical comfort of the cast.

CASTING

It is a lucky director who can stage a production with experienced puppeteers, but opportunities to do so are rare. Most often the cast members will be volunteers, students, or recruits who have little or no background in puppetry or theatre. The challenge is to transform these individuals of diverse interests and abilities into an ensemble of able animators.

I like to spend one or two prerehearsal sessions in putting a group through some of the games and exercises described in Chapter III. This introduces everyone to the general concepts of puppeteering, and defines the problems for the type of figure they will handle. The sessions should be informal and fun, to ease tensions about what lies ahead. The exercises are done without puppets to keep the emphasis on persons and problem-solving skills. As cast members begin to think independently about puppetry, they become contributors to the creative process. I welcome suggestions and ideas from a cast, because their commitment to a production grows as their personal participation increases. Exciting theatre grows out of performers who are knowledgeable, enthusiastic, and involved.

Designer-director George Latshaw is dwarfed by the 9-foot puppets he created for Billy the Kid, *a commission from the Detroit Institute of Arts in 1958 for performances with the Detroit Symphony. It was shown at Ford Auditorium, with a seating capacity of 3,000.*

The training program is also a quick way to generate a group spirit through the shared learning experience. Once a group identity emerges, it can be nurtured into a sense of ensemble for the performance. It is important that each person feel capable; that each person respect the skills of the others; and that all persons recognize the collective impact they can have in working together. Out of this loose beginning, I start to make decisions on casting so that the strengths of each individual will have a chance to shine.

First Reading Rehearsal

After roles are assigned, the director discusses the interpretation of the work to be staged. General comments on characterization, scene objectives, and special manipulating problems are included. This is an outline of the work to be done. Each puppeteer will listen for the broad view, as well as for clues to the interpretation of the assigned role. A first reading may raise questions, which can be answered on the spot. If the production is for a symphony concert, the music serves as the text for the mimed action and choreography to come. It helps to run through text or music several times, so that it is familiar, before moving on to the blocking.

The cast is usually eager to handle the puppets they will use in performance, and they need an unstructured time to get acquainted with the figures and controls. They have been exposed to the concepts, so the freedom to experiment with a puppet, to find out what it can do, is important to their continuing education in puppetry. The more the puppeteers can discover on their own, the less they will have to be told later on. They should

The music for Aaron Copland's Billy the Kid Suite *was the "text" for the production. Memorizing the music and learning to handle the giants occurred simultaneously during blocking rehearsals.*

The Emperor's New Clothes, *produced by the Pacific Conservatory of the Performing Arts, Santa Maria, Calif., in 1969. Shown are members of the acting company working overhead from a seated position on rolling stools. The director must watch the two-level traffic of both puppets and puppeteers.*

Scene: The Loom Room, as Snippolino and Pasghetti, two actors posing as tailors, plan to make a fool of the Emperor, who did not want to see their show. The audience sees only the action on the puppet stage level.

be allowed to work at random as long as it is fun and productive. The mechanics of blocking at the next rehearsal will change the mood sharply.

Blocking—Two-level Traffic

A blocking rehearsal defines the setting, the acting space, and the movement within that space. The director blocks in the movement for the puppet in its stage space with an eye to its effect on the puppeteers attached to the puppet in an offstage space. No masking is used during the blocking and early rehearsals so the director can observe the flow of action in both areas.

Novice puppeteers should have the stage areas (upstage, downstage) identified for them, as well as directions (to their left and right). A quick rundown on basic body positions (full front, quarter turn, profile, face in,

face out, etc.) helps them to understand the director's instructions.

Each type of puppet has its own stage space. The black theatre and the Bunraku style use the full stage of the actor's theatre. A ground plan, marked with masking tape, serves as a guide to entrances and exits and wall space on the set. If open stage animation is used for a symphony concert, the playing area in front of the orchestra will be shallow, so the cast should become accustomed to working within marked limits right from the start.

Stages for hand puppets and marionettes are confining in their own ways. Generally the playing area is quite broad but not very deep, so the blocking will have to be inventive to minimize the flat effect of the working area.

Since it is difficult to manage both puppet and script at the same time, blocking notations may be put on the scripts without puppets.

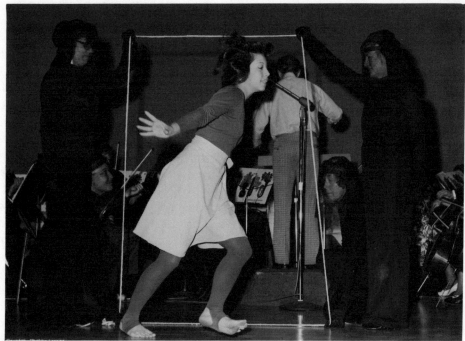

PHOTO: GARY BOYNTON

The Pemrad Puppets Bicentennial Project, directed by George Latshaw, with the Lansing Symphony. The limits of stage space were defined during rehearsals for this scene with four puppeteers and a dancer. At the technical rehearsal, when this photograph was taken, the orchestra setup, the conductor's podium, and the microphone stand took away even more space. The performers adjusted well because rehearsals had dealt with variables in performance conditions.

Then, without scripts, try the action with puppets as someone reads along to provide the cues. Set action a scene at a time, or as much as the group can assimilate in a session. The director must decide how much or how little detail to give. It is better to confine the blocking rehearsal to broad movement patterns, crosses, entrances, and exits. Save the details until after lines are learned, or the cast will become so discouraged by the monumental task of remembering everything that the session will not be productive.

A stage cross is a simple thing for an actor to accomplish, but for the marionette operator it may be a major production if it requires passing in front of another puppet and puppeteer. To get past the intervening puppeteer, the one making the cross will have to step behind the obstacle, holding the control in one hand, encircle the puppeteer, pick up the control in the other hand, and continue the cross; or the puppeteers may trade controllers.

The director will discover that these are the difficult moves:

On marionette bridge—One figure crossing another.
Overhead (hand or rod)—Puppeteers tend to face full front, and they take up more space in the shoulder-to-shoulder position. If the puppets are to stand close together, suggest that the puppeteers stand profile so that they take up less room, and the puppets can be in the correct position. The puppeteer working overhead does not always have to assume the same position underneath the stage as the puppet above.
On stools, working overhead—Knees and stools will take up space, so the offstage traffic patterns and body positions may have to be adjusted to help the puppets above maintain the right relationships.

Another thing that may inhibit puppet action is the unspoken social distance we preserve in our relationships with other people. Body contact between puppeteers cannot be avoided, because their bulk is so much greater than the puppets they are controlling. Once the cast overcomes its awkwardness about touching (through the exercises in Chapter III), the puppet movement will improve.

PHYSICAL STRAIN

The director should be aware of the physical strain involved in certain types of manipulation and allow for frequent breaks in the early rehearsals. Cast morale can be maintained by working in small segments at first and gradually increasing their duration as stamina increases. Rehearsals are the "spring training camp" periods for puppeteers, when they build their physical conditioning to get ready for the season. Overhead manipulation is not a skill that anyone brings to a first rehearsal, nor is bending over a backdrop rail with arms outstretched on a marionette bridge. A sympathetic director will be prepared for complaints about aching arms, backs, and shoulders and will suggest ways to ease the muscle strain.

My first job as a hand puppeteer was for Wallace Puppets of New York City. I had manipulated hand puppets, but never in the overhead position while seated on a rolling stool. My stool was very low to the ground to reduce my height of 6'4", and I found it difficult to get the leverage to move it around. When I put both hands in the air, I was immobilized. Bill Tennent, the director and company manager, told me that the secret was to raise the arms high and close to the head, and lock them in at the shoulder socket. I tried it but could not maintain the position for any length of time. As I tried to relax, my arms would sag, then shake, and finally drop. It was a very stop-and-go rehearsal, and at the end of the first day I thought I would die. After a week of rehearsal we took off to play a summer camp in the mountains. By this time I was able to keep my arms up for the entire show and remember my lines, if little else. One scene required me to make an exit with puppets on both hands. To move the stool, I gave

Billy the Kid. *Puppeteers develop stamina during rehearsal so they can turn their attention to the refinements of ensemble playing.*

a sharp thrust with my bottom, and fell off. The puppets sagged momentarily, recovered and walked off, as I made the exit on my knees. I had learned not to let down until completely offstage. In two months I was able to keep my arms in the air for an hour's performance with no strain at all and could give my attention to detailed manipulation.

RUNNING REHEARSALS

Rehearsals become more interesting after the mechanics of blocking, business, and lines are out of the way. The puppeteers can concentrate on characterization and interaction to make the play come alive. When this work begins, the cast deserves to hear praise for the progress it makes.

Directors differ in their methods of working with people. Some few shout and rage when things do not go right. They intimidate the cast, defying them to do better in order to avoid further tantrums. Other directors are such inventive eager-beavers that they jump up on stage, grab the puppets, and show "how" it ought to be done. The puppeteers are turned into robots, programmed to do only what the director tells them. Another approach helps performers to be more productive, I believe.

It is not always necessary to "tell" everything if a well-phrased question could produce the same result.

What is the character feeling in this scene? What would that emotion do to the body—
  the voice?

How can your puppet show that to the audience?

Trusting people to think, enabling them to make discoveries, welcoming them into the creative process of a production are ways to enrich the results for the participants and for the audience. When cast members are helped to feel clever and inventive, everyone benefits —including the director, for the performers will carry the show on stage. The "can do" attitude is good for morale.

The Bear Who Played the Bijou was a prize play in a contest sponsored by The Detroit Institute of Arts. Michigan artist Charles Culver was commissioned to design the production, and special music was composed for it. I was invited to direct the cast of Junior League volunteers, who were new to puppetry. In one scene, the bear of the title and a boy who befriended him were required to paddle across the stage in a canoe. Each puppeteer struggled to hold up a puppet and clench a paddle at the same time. When I asked them to hold up the ends of the canoe with their free hands, their response was, "Impossible!" They had never handled anything like it before, so, of course, it seemed impossible. By working on the actions separately, they found they could put the two pieces together easily. The action of paddling had one rhythm, the lilt of the canoe another, and they made it very convincing that the canoe was afloat on water. Later I was told that any new stage business that seemed beyond reach at first sight was given a cast password—"*Cope!*" A sense of humor helped them cope in splendid fashion—and they discovered that by trying, they could also say, "Can do!" Their polished performance at the premiere was a source of pride to all of us.

CHECK LIST

1) Do the puppeteers make eye contact with each other, or have they learned to transfer their full attention to the stage so that the dialogue is on a puppet-to-puppet basis.

2) Are movement characterizations progressing? Does each puppet move and react in an individual way?

3) Are vocal characterizations emerging? Is there enough contrast between voices? Are the words clear and easy to hear? Is it obvious which puppet is speaking at all times?

4) Do the listening puppets focus on the speaker with their heads and eyes? This helps the audience to know which puppet has the line.

5) It is a convention in the puppet theatre that only the speaking puppet moves. Are the other puppets respecting this need for focus? Movement for reaction must be inserted between sentences or speeches. It seems artificial at first, but it helps the audience to follow the action selectively without distraction.

6) Does the impulse for movement seem to come from inside the puppet, or is it obviously an external force jerking and pulling the puppet into positions?

7) Are the puppets doing interesting things to watch, or do they stand around and talk a lot?

8) Are the puppets believable? Have they taken on a life of their own? Are the scenes believable?

9) Is there a sense of timing within the scenes and a rhythm and pace to the whole production?

Although puppeteers have an angled view of what they are doing, beginners frequently comment that they have no idea what their work looks like from the audience. If they could see their own work (not just a substitute doing it for them, or a director describing it), it would be a revelation. If it is possible to videotape scenes, the playback can be tremendously beneficial to the cast. A more effective performance by the puppet and more sensitive manipulation are the rewards when the puppeteers are allowed to evaluate their own work.

Even after the scenes are put together and

the players are learning to sustain a performance, the director should be watchful for signs of strain. Hand puppeteers sometimes rest the base of the puppet against the playboard to help support weary arm muscles. Gradually the puppet tilts to a 45-degree angle and looks like a human fly. If the puppets are kept away from the playboard, it cannot be used as a rest-stop during performance. Hand puppeteers also relax the wrist by letting it fall back, and this gives the puppet the appearance of a pelvic thrust with head gazing into the sky. Keep puppets erect with eyes focused on the action.

The marionette is subject to sagging and slump when the manipulator rests elbows on the leaning rail. No part of the stage should become a prop for the puppeteer. The marionette should have both feet on the floor in a proper stance, but there may be times when it floats off the ground in a levitation not called for by the script. The Groucho Marx lope with bent knees is another effect that may crop up when the manipulator is tired.

Rod puppets have to be watched so that their heads are focused on the action. Shadow puppets need a director on the other side of the screen to check the sharpness of the full image and the control of movement and effects.

TECH REHEARSALS

The technical aspects of production are usually dealt with during the rehearsal period and will not require a special session. Puppet companies handle their own sound, lights, and scene shifts, which is more efficient for them than the theatre practice of calling in separate crews.

Sets. Do they serve their purpose without being cumbersome, and without competing with the puppets? Can the scene shifts be done swiftly?

Lights. Are the puppets sufficiently illuminated to see without strain? If there is mood lighting, will the audience be able to follow the characters and action? The puppet prosce-

COURTESY WALLACE D. HUSKONEN, EXECUTIVE PRODUCER, PENTON/IPC FILMS DIVISION

The Magic of Cycolac, *a Borg-Warner promotional film, starred an animated cartoon Wizard. For a short sequence, this three-dimensional puppet of the Wizard was used. Movements were confined to a given camera field, so the cameraman arranged a mirror below camera level for the puppeteers to monitor during the shooting. Manipulation was to playback of voice track on tape. Puppeteers George Latshaw (above) and Chris Latshaw (below) were dressed in invisible black behind the lighted area for the Wizard puppet. "Wiz" character and design copyrighted by Rick Reinert Productions.*

nium is often a small window of light in a vast darkened auditorium. When the lighting remains dim for a prolonged period, the audience may be lulled by the soft, night-light effect and fall asleep. What compromise can be worked out between visibility and mood?

Sound. For live voices, check levels, clarity, and projection. For taped voice and music tracks, is there clear sound without distortion? What is the best level of sound before it seems "amplified"?

Setup and Strike. If the production is portable, the cast should be assigned tasks for putting up and taking down the stage, sound

Pushbutton Planet, *produced by the Pacific Conservatory of the Performing Arts in 1969, and directed by George Latshaw. Two-person manipulating teams developed skill in managing both the puppet and the space capsule in which it traveled.*

equipment, and lights and packing puppets, sets, and props.

DRESS REHEARSAL

This should be smooth sailing in a puppet production, for the technical elements do not arrive at the last minute to disrupt everything as they do in the theatre. Makeup and costume have been on since the first rehearsal, the sets are no surprise, and there has been light and sound to rehearse by. Final rehearsals can be devoted to polishing and playing it. At this point it should be ready for a preview of audience reaction.

When the director feels the production is ready, he will turn it over to the cast, so they can take full responsibility for the performance they have built together. Some notes on early performances may be useful reminders of dealing with audiences. The rehearsal period

may develop such a sense of ensemble that the cast is able to cope with any audience situation it encounters. It is a happy moment for the director to watch a good cast standing on its own.

To assist the nontheatre person in understanding what a director does to develop meaningful and exciting stage picturization, the following exercise may be useful.

Exercise #1—Stop-action Sequence with Live Actors

Comic strips tell a story in a sequence of frames. Each frame or drawing shows a highlight of the action as it progresses to a conclusion. In this exercise think of a story (don't copy a comic strip or cartoon) that you can show in a sequence of 5 to 8 "frames" that freeze the action. What the observers see each time is a static pose, a tableau. There are no words, sound effects, or movements within the frame. To see only the "frame," the observers must close their eyes and only open them on cue from the performing group when they are in position. Allow several seconds for the observers to view the frame, call "close," and move into position for next frame. Repeat to conclusion.

This is a good exercise for following dramatic action, checking on changing relationships within the scene, and discovering through changes in movement what has happened in the story. Examples:

Little Nell tied to the railroad tracks and rescued.

Casey at the Bat goes down to defeat.

Bank holdup foiled by old-lady customer.

Exercise #2—Stop-action Sequence with Puppets

Take a key scene from a play and "show" it in five to eight frame stop-action sequence. Is there the same degree of variety in these scenes as there was with live performers? If not, why not? What can puppets do to make dramatic and compelling stage pictures? Is there too much reliance on puppet dialogue to explain rather than "show" action?

Chapter XIII

PERFORMANCE AND THE AUDIENCE

A puppeteer's performance is divided into three time periods that extend beyond the actual time on stage. These are:

1) Arrival and setup
2) Performance (onstage time)
3) Strike and load

It is well to consider all three as performance schedule, so that energy can be conserved and expended at the proper times.

Preplanning can assist the smooth flow of the arrival and setup. Most information on requirements would be covered in the correspondence leading to a contract, but it is wise to refresh the memory of the sponsor with an arrival reminder card or letter. This courtesy arriving five days prior to performance assures the sponsor of the company's reliability, and can be a checklist of requirements on the site.

This communication should include:

The day, date, hour, and location of performance.
The title of the program to be presented and running time.
The expected hour of arrival in advance for setup.
Any special unloading instructions.

Requirements:
Unloading assistance—one, two, three persons to carry.
Stage space to be occupied by puppet setup.
The number and kind of electrical outlets required. (It is wise to carry your own 50′ heavy-duty extension.)

Dressing room, if necessary.
Work table, if needed for props, sound, etc.
Stage masking.
Special assistance in handling house lights, or other cues.
Repeat request for carry-out assistance and strike time required.
Sound equipment—it is better to carry your own.

The reminder can pave the way for a warm welcome and smooth entry into the theatre space. There is nothing more traumatic for sponsor and performer than to have last-minute demands on arrival for conditions that cannot be met at that late hour. Clear the way, and in most cases everything will be ready for your appearance.

A puppeteer's nightmare is to arrive at the unloading dock and find all the doors on that side of the building locked; the persons to help unload do not show up; it is 40 below and the only entrance is through an outside fire escape that is a glaze of ice. That nightmare gives one a quick evaluation of the size, shape, and weight of the equipment. How easy is it to carry? How many trips would one person, working alone, have to make to get it inside? Would a portable dolly or loading rack be a good thing to have along for emergencies?

The setup is the moment of truth, when you ask yourself if there is not some more sensible way to make a living. Keep calm, and get as much help as possible on the physical lifting, carrying, placement, etc. Save your energy for the performance. If band practice left the chairs up, if the chorus risers are still

Preperformance schedule includes unloading the van.

Consider using a dolly to reduce the time it takes to move in.

in place, if the school play is in rehearsal and you can't get into the wings because the gym equipment is stored there, if the light board is locked and no one can find the work lights, keep calm. Delegate responsibility, get a runner, and get help.

When meeting with the contact person at the theatre, recheck your requirements and state the exact time you will be ready to have the house open and the audience brought in. Confirm the starting time, and ask where emergency help may be located if that person is not staying. Then go about your business.

You learn to appreciate an efficient puppet stage that goes up easily. This is no time to wrestle with equipment or get angry when devices don't work properly. If you have rehearsed the setup as well as the production, you have discovered shortcuts to save your strength for performance. Wasted moves only

wear you out before you go on—but a good setup can serve as a "warm-up" with the bending, stretching, and reaching involved in the task. Some persons need a half-hour break between setup and show to be performance-ready; others gain zest from finishing the setup backstage as the audience comes in and can move into the show on the accumulated steam. Sound and light checks should be made from the house before the audience arrives.

There are a number of preperformance decisions that may affect your success with the audience. These include considerations of the size of the audience, the locale (interior or exterior), and the age range admitted.

Size of Audience

Be fair to yourself in determining the scale on which you can play to best advantage. A show that may be perfect for an intimate setting of 250 will be lost in a coliseum that seats 1,500. It is not fair to the performer, sponsor, or audience to oversell and be swallowed up in a barn. If people cannot see well and cannot hear well, they may cool to the whole idea of puppet shows, yours and all the others that might come after. If necessary, limit your audience. You may lose a few dates, but you will have respect from the

PHOTO: DICK JOHNSON

The setup is no time to wrestle with the equipment.

PHOTO: DICK JOHNSON

Appreciate a stage that goes up one-two-three.

PHOTO: DICK JOHNSON

Use setup time to stretch and warm up for the performance.

PHOTO: DICK JOHNSON

The puppet stage as seen from the front. Allow time to put speakers in place and make a sound and light check from the house before the audience arrives.

ones you do book for your style, your show, and your sense of what is appropriate. Be intimate with your audience, if that is your forte.

LOCALE

Sometimes the puppet show must be done outdoors for a recreation program, company picnic, or summer camp setting. Be concerned with comfortable seating. Sometimes sprawling on the grass is preferable to backless benches or hard folding chairs. What will give you the best sound coverage and sightlines in the situation? Be prepared for competition from the great outdoors—the passing plane, the bird on the wing, a squirrel up a tree, the friendly dogs, the changing clouds. Anything can happen outside!

The wind can be an unexpected factor to cope with. Will the drapes or masking for the booth stay in place, or will they fly up revealing the backstage area? Can the stage stand up to a stiff breeze? What happens when a marionette faces headwinds and cannot stay on the ground?

The bright sunshine may pour into the booth and light up the puppeteer behind the scrim. To keep the backstage in shadow, carry a masking to cover the top and back of the booth. This will keep out the light and convert the stage into a sauna. It is useful to wear a sweat band and to dust arms and hands with talcum powder to ease getting in and out of hand puppets during the sticky season.

Expect a curious child to wander around behind you to get a better look at what is going on. This sets up a second show, for the audience finds it hilarious to watch the child's reaction to the peep-show view backstage. Try to handle the situation quickly and graciously, so that the child will return to the audience; puppets cannot compete while the real-life drama is going on. When there is any doubt about the weather, request an alternate setup that is protected, or have a standby crew alerted to shift your setup to shelter in case of rain.

AGE OF AUDIENCE

"For children from 6 to 60" and "Fun for all" are advertising slogans used to suggest that there are few or no limits to the ages that will be entranced by puppets. These catch phrases spell disaster for the company presenting an adult production, for some parents simply will not believe that there are any age restrictions connected with puppetry. The babe-in-arms who cries relentlessly or the preschool child who has to have everything explained can be as disturbing at a children's play as they are out of place in an adult audience. Do you really want to play to everyone from the cradle to the grave, or could you do a better job by reserving your services for the school age or older? It will take firm and tactful education of parents and public before the wisdom of "no one under (?) admitted" will be accepted. Pornography serves a limited clientele; why not puppetry, which might have some redeeming social values?

PRECONDITIONED MEDIA AUDIENCES

Movie matinees and home television viewing have conditioned audience behavior toward the casual and away from the formal occasion of times past. A professional performer must reckon with these influences. For children, the movie is a social event, seeing and being seen, munching popcorn, moving around freely. The film rolls on whether anyone is attentive or not. Television's stop-and-go segments allow for even more peripheral activity in a cycle of fragmented action separated by commercial breaks. Is it any wonder that today's audiences find it difficult to concentrate on the sustained continuity of a live performance? Even professional children's theatre has turned to the musical version of everything, with songs and dances serving as the commercial breaks, whether they have anything to do with the plot or not. An audience has to sacrifice some individuality to be a member of a group in a public place, and there are few models to prepare the young for this experience. A talk about "theatre manners" before the play is a late attempt to catch up. The best solution to this problem is to admit parents and children together. They have the fun of sharing an experience, and the parent can serve as a model for what is appropriate behavior for the occasion.

SCHEDULING

The success of a puppet show depends on the timing, not only in the performance, but also on the hour in the day's schedule. A performance during school time has relatively few problems, for the discipline of the school covers the situation. After-school performances are another matter, for without the accustomed break at the end of the school day, children will feel the show delays their needed release. This is the least favorable time to schedule anything but wide-open playtime outdoors.

Saturday performances can be set for morning or afternoon, and just before or after the lunch hour seems a convenient time for parents. An early evening performance on a Friday is also suitable for a young audience if it fits the pattern of community activities.

COMFORT AND CONTROL

The comfort of the audience should be a concern to the performer, for viewers cannot give their attention to being entertained if they are busy looking after personal needs. Being too warm is a problem summer and winter. All those bodies in close contact can turn up the thermostat. For comfort, the audience should be on the cool side. Although these are matters for the house staff and the building engineers, the performer should be aware of conditions that will get the show off to a good start. The noise of heating or cooling devices should be eliminated during a performance. Food and drink inside the theatre should be a "no-no," and printed programs serve no purpose for the young except as paper airplanes. In a school show, suggest that the lower grades

be brought in last, for the anticipation of first and second graders is so great that they should have the shortest wait. In a gym-auditorium, it is possible to seat the children on mats or on the floor. It is difficult to reach an audience across the Great Gulf of Basketball Court to the bleacher seating on the far shore.

OPEN HOUSE

A children's audience can find seats and fill a house in fifteen minutes or less. Early arrivals who have an hour to kill before the show should do it outside where they can move around. The less time spent in waiting, the better.

Some children enter a public building as if they had been invited to an indoor track meet. They run relay races between their seats and the bathroom or drinking fountain, touching all bases before the next round. This sparks a competitive interest in their neighbors and may lead to a race to see who can do it the most times. Musical chairs or "Let's trade seats" is another waiting game. Clock-watching is played by everyone who can tell time.

A musical interlude or overture is sometimes used to keep the restless natives at bay before show time. The surrounding sound that today's young generation uses via radio or television indicates that sound is preferable to silence, even if it does not command attention.

Start on time! Waiting for the last bus to arrive is like trying to hold down the Apollo launch vehicle after the zero countdown. It is already too late to change, the audience is ready to blast off, and it is time to go. No lectures, announcements, or introductions should interfere. Don't tinker with their time by perpetuating the theatrical myth that "shows never start on time anyway."

PERFORMANCE

Warm-ups or Direct Entry

If you haven't already sized up the audience to some degree by their behavior and sound

Backstage: Listening to the audience assemble can give some clues as to what is in store.

level before the play, you will have your chance the moment the house lights dim. Your personal style will decide whether to proceed directly into the play. If you have an informal touch and wish to explore the audience through a series of preliminary variety turns, this approach can be fun. Audience participation can be a delight or disaster, depending on whether it is direct or indirect, and whether the "participation" is fresh and genuine or the same, old, tired thing that everyone has been through dozens of times.

There is a standard bit that sets my teeth on edge. It is called "Hello, Jerry." The puppet appears and shouts to the audience, "Hello, boys and girls." The voice is not quite as shrill as Punch but has a somewhat nasty edge to it. When the audience response is moderate, the puppet berates them to shout his name louder and louder until the building vibrates

and the walls crack. Any puppeteer who meets an audience of strangers, treats them like a mob, and incites them to riot deserves all the difficulties that will follow. Children are direct. If you ask them a question, they will give an answer. It is not always the same answer, or the "expected" answer, but they will reply. Participation is only one measure of audience response. There are other ways to win them, if you treat them with respect.

FEEDBACK FROM HECKLERS

A performer always has the option of ignoring smart remarks or giving the unruly the attention that they seek. Any acknowledgment may be interpreted as a cue to continue, and you end up with a running battle on your hands. If you have a lightning wit and hear the right kind of feeder line from the enemy, try to end it with a ZAP. Don't engage in a skirmish, or you will find the control of the performance has moved from the stage to the audience. If you are unsure, ignore the hecklers and maybe they will go away with or without an usher's help.

I once played a show for a Family Night at a country club. The children had finished the meal long before the adults were served coffee and dessert, and the youngsters began to wander away from the tables. I heard one father take a stab at keeping his child occupied. "Count all the red ties in the room," he instructed, and the answer came back in a flash. "Now count all the red bow ties," continued the dad, warming to the inventiveness of the game. The unseen computer child had the answer to that one in no time, and I waited to see what the topper would be. There was none. The father had run out of ideas. By this time more children were milling around trying to stir up the adults so the show would start. A leisurely time later, I was allowed to begin.

When the stage lights went up, there was a cheer. The first puppet appeared, and there was a burst of laughter. The puppet moved, and everybody guffawed. I began to realize with some horror that the audience and I were vying for equal time. The youngsters were so wound up from waiting so long that they were overresponding to the slightest move. The duration of their response was killing any sense of pace. I proceeded with the opening sketch called "Wilbur Builds a Puppet." In this routine, Wilbur, a pert youngster with a shock of red hair, finds a book with instructions for creating a simple puppet from a hand, a handkerchief, and a styrofoam ball. It was one of my favorite numbers, and I was not looking forward to playing it against the roar of the crowd. While I was searching for a way to handle it, the audience came up with the clue.

Wilbur had just looked in the book for the next step, and had announced, "Now I'm going to need a hand!" A voice from the audience piped up, "I've got a hand," and other voices picked up the phrase until everyone had had a turn, and another voice topped it with "I've got TWO hands!" Wilbur began to perk up. "Do you ALL have two hands?" he asked, and a solid chorus yelled back "Yes!" "Good," snapped Wilbur, "then put them over your mouth and SHUT UP!" There was a moment of stunned silence, a ripple of nervous chuckles from the adults, and then a satisfying hush. The kids had been zapped and they knew it. They settled down, we were friends, and the show moved on without a hitch.

I really do not advocate using blunt language with an audience, but in this case it worked after a split second to decide if it was worth the risk. It was necessary to scoop the children up all at once, to have them all answer the same question at the same time, so they would all hear the POW that would set things straight. This audience walked right into the setup, and Wilbur delivered the punch.

In general, I feel that ad lib is a siren call that has lured many a tongue to a shattering end. Ad libs are for emergency use only (whether solo or group) unless the performers are well trained and gifted in the improvisational technique. Trying to ad lib a total show is beyond the skill of most of us. An occasional ad lib retort as embellishment or embroidery

to a set script can be the proof that the theatre is alive and unique for each audience each time.

The Backstage Watch

It is a good idea to have timed the show by segments during the rehearsal period, so that during a performance a watch can tell you if you are racing, lagging, or right on time. If you have a deadline—a 45-minute show—are you at the right spot at that moment? Could you cut—simplify—jump without leaving out essentials? When you are secure in playing a show, time adjustments can be made with ease. No need to run short or to run long. Run right on time.

Curtain Calls

For a children's audience, I prefer to let the puppets take the bows to retain some of the mystery and illusion of the piece. For older groups, I do take a bow to satisfy their curiosity about the person behind the scenes. A human popping out on a puppet stage can bring a gasp from the audience, for the illusion created by the puppets makes their scale seem human, and the puppeteer appears to be a giant.

Some puppeteers take a curtain call and then do an encore by stripping the masking from the puppet stage and repeating a scene to expose how it was done. This can be instructive or anticlimactic, depending on how it is handled. What memory do you want to leave?

After the Show

The experience of playing a show can vary from exhilaration, to let-down, to exhaustion. The energy and concentration required to sustain an hour's performance using eight to twelve characters and being "on" for the entire time can tax the most physically conditioned person. For the puppeteer the performance is not finished until the show is packed and loaded in the vehicle. The strike can be the physical wind-down from the tension of performance.

Backstage Visitors

One of the pleasant rewards is having people come backstage after the show. Various companies have set policies on who may come and how many may come. Some prefer to have no one backstage; others welcome everybody. Between the two extremes there are special groups who may request a visit or simply drop in. Cub Scouts and Brownie Troops need to see a show and talk to the puppeteer as a partial requirement for a badge in puppetry. There may be local or area puppeteers, for news of a show travels like wildfire, and puppeteers are the most avid fans of the art, traveling miles to see a show. Youngsters with puppets of their own to show may come back for a word of advice and encouragement.

If you are wise, you will take advantage of your "carry out" help as soon as you have taken your bow. Don't let them slip away while you chat, but have tasks to assign. They can coil electrical cable, position the packing cases, wind the speaker cords. If you know what to do, what to delegate, to keep the flow going, you can enjoy visitors at the same time the show is coming down. Any show mess, broken balloons, tissue paper, confetti, scraps can be scooped up by your helpers. Packed cases and trunks can be carried to the exit, so the equipment is ready to load the moment the last bundle is wrapped and the stage is down.

Until you know the show by heart, a packing list can be useful to double-check that everything is returned to the right space. It would be shrewd to pack puppets and special props yourself. Some visitors cannot resist the

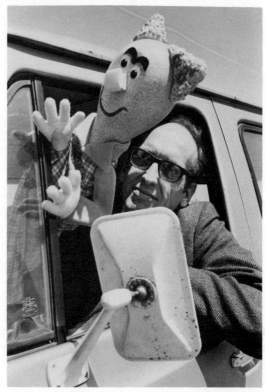

PHOTO: DICK JOHNSON

The performance is not over until the gear is back in the van and it's time to wave goodbye.

urge to touch the puppets, and you may counter by saying, "I'll be glad to show you as I pack them." Countless hands can leave their mark, so it is not unreasonable to protect the freshness of the puppet. One does not ask to try on the actors' costumes in the dressing room, and the puppet is just as personal a part of the puppeteer's disguise.

The performance cycle is not really over, until the load is in the car, and you are ready to wave goodbye to the helpers as you drive away.

Chapter XIV

CAREERS

When I first expressed an interest in puppetry as a career, outsiders derisively referred to the field as "playing with dolls." They rated puppeteering a cut below being an actor and not a fit profession for adults, although Tony Sarg, The Yale Puppeteers, Helen Joseph, Rufus Rose, and others were visibly successful at the time. Puppetry in the mid-1940's was still considered a novelty, too limited in appeal to support more than the few who were already at the top.

Even after television showed millions that puppetry could be an art as well as an occupation, doubt lingered in the public mind. Every traveling puppeteer has heard the same three questions repeated in every town in every state. They are: "What do you do for a living?", "Is this what you do full time?" and "How did you get started with puppets?" The idea of being self-supporting in a field that one so obviously enjoys seems to be an incredible work/life-style combination to the people who ask. It is an unbeatable combination for puppeteers.

For all-you-ever-wanted-to-know-about-puppeteers-but-didn't-know-whom-to-ask, join The Puppeteers of America, Inc. Membership is open to all persons of any age, interest, or experience. The lively, bimonthly issues of *The Puppetry Journal,* the Consulting Services, and the week-long national festivals will give you a vivid picture of the field in short order. At the annual festivals, information flows freely, for the experts are generous in sharing their know-how. The future of their art hinges on their ability to inform, encourage, and inspire the best in the people who will carry on. A be-

ginner can meet and mingle face-to-face with puppeteers of national and international renown, and also with puppeteers of matching age and experience. During the festival performances, the strong "family" feeling of the organization emerges. The success of one member on stage is wildly celebrated by all the "relatives" in the audience, for it means their mutual art is in good and capable hands. A puppeteer can receive no better send-off than to have the "family" approve and applaud the work.

Women have played such a major role in the renaissance of puppetry in the United States that it seems redundant to mention that they have been the equals of men from the pioneering days of the 1920's. Women have been contributors to all aspects of the field: as researchers, bibliographers, book authors, experimenters, playwrights, performers, producers, designers, directors, manufacturers, and educators. Puppetry in the United States was "liberated" forty years before women's lib surfaced as a national movement.

The individual searching for employment as a puppeteer may find that the economic picture of the wooden world is a many-splintered thing. The opportunities to work as an apprentice or journeyman for a professional company are extremely limited. Temporary jobs for puppeteers center on special projects (television, industrial shows) or short seasonal bookings (summer and Christmas seasons). The difficulty of breaking in and continuing with an established company tends to perpetuate the puppeteer's singular approach.

One person can be self-employed and sur-

144

COURTESY JEAN WIKSELL   COURTESY OLGA STEVENS   HARMON STUDIO

(Left) *Jean Starr Wiksell, first woman President of Puppeteers of America and long-time Puppetry Consultant for the Association of Junior Leagues.* (Center) *Olga Stevens, Executive Secretary of the P. of A (1948 photo shows rod puppets from* Macbeth). (Right) *Rachel Redinger, founder of "Trumpet in the Land" outdoor historical drama at New Philadelphia, Ohio; P. of A. Director of Media Development, and guiding spirit of the new North American Puppet Theatre Foundation.*

COURTESY ARCHIE ELLIOTT   COURTESY
GAYLE MICHAEL ANDERSON   BOYNTON PHOTOGRAPHY

(Left) *Archie Elliott, twice P. of A. President and continuing Festival Coordinator.* (Center) *The late Vivian Michael, Editor of* The Puppetry Journal *(1960–69) and manager of The Puppetry Store until 1971.* (Right) *Don Avery, the innovative Editor (since 1969) of* The Puppetry Journal.

COURTESY MOLLIE FALKENSTEIN   COURTESY NAT EEK

(Left) *Mollie Falkenstein (in costume as Mother Goose), Second Vice President of UNIMA and Secretary of UNIMA-USA.* (Right) *Nat Eek, Dean of the College of Fine Arts, University of Oklahoma; President of the international children's theatre organization ASSITEJ (1972–75); Director of the Drama School's Agamemnon with giant puppets while Department Head.*

vive—even managing a comfortable sort of gypsy life. Husband and wife teams flourish by keeping it all in the family. Two-person partnerships also pool business and artistic skills for a share of the profits. To expand beyond two persons is to invite all the problems of a professional performing arts organization where miracle workers are needed to meet the rising costs. A few entrepreneurs do manage to maintain resident or touring companies of modest size, but the United States has nothing to compare with the scale of the state-supported theatres of Central Europe. There, the puppet theatre serves an important educational function, which is both artistic and political. It receives the budget and the personnel to carry out this work with style. In Russia, Poland, Czechoslovakia, Hungary, and Rumania, puppet companies are housed in their own theatre buildings with a staff of up to fifty or more specialists. The resulting productions are more expansive in execution than what can be mounted commercially in America.

The puppeteer who does not wish to be a solo performer may have to devise ingenious methods for mounting large-scale productions with a group. Financing is a major problem. Some puppeteers may have a cause to which volunteers will rally, as the Bread and Puppet Theatre did with its antiwar protest plays. Others have used the barter system to acquire the services for a big show (San Francisco Bay Area puppeteers). Any member producer could call on others in the talent pool to be manipulators, voices, scriptwriters, designers, and builders to meet his or her project requirements. These periodic exchanges benefited everyone in a sort of rotating repertory system.

In other regions of the country, an experienced puppeteer could search for an enlightened drama department in a college or university. The school can provide assistance in the form of a residency for the "guest puppeteer" who is qualified to teach. Such arrangements include a stipend, the time and budget for the production, a student cast to perform the work, an audience to view it, and a critical review of the result.

The community arts organization is another possible source for underwriting a commissioned work. A cast of volunteer-trainees often makes up in zeal what it lacks in experience, and this momentum can build the skills necessary for an effective performance. Several of these one-time opportunities in scattered locales can build the confidence and continuity necessary for the artistic growth of the puppeteer.

An independent puppeteer can pursue the will-o'-the-wisp of "nonprofit" status in order to apply for government grants, arts council assistance, and foundation support. The truth is that puppeteers will be asked to stand at the end of the line behind the symphony orchestras, the art museums, the regional theatres, and the dance companies that are also tapping these same sources to survive.

Although television has been a major force in popularizing puppetry, it has not changed the age-old patterns of the itinerant showmen and women who go on the road to reach their audiences. Resident puppet theatres in a few major cities are trying to reverse the trend by establishing a home base where audiences can come to see puppets in a season of plays.

Theatrical unions cover most of the entertainment world, and puppeteers must join a union to work professionally in these fields.

Actors Equity—Live actors and puppeteers on the legitimate stage.

American Guild of Variety Artists (AGVA) —Entertainers who have "acts" (booked through agents) for shopping malls, cruise ships, club dates, music halls, etc.

American Federation of Television and Radio Artists (AFTRA)—Commercial television programs (local and network), videotaped commercials, puppet voices for radio spots, etc.

Screen Actors Guild (SAG)—Motion pictures, film-strips, industrial films, etc.

Writers Guild of America, East/West— Puppet scriptwriters for television, films, etc.

Theatrical agents earn a 10 percent (and sometimes higher) commission on talent fees above scale (the minimum payment established by the union for a specified job). Variety puppeteers work through many agents on a nonexclusive basis. The "act" provides the promotional material (résumés, brochures, glossy photographs, press releases) for an agent. The agent books the dates, writes the contracts, collects the fees, and pays the talent. A "franchised" theatrical agent is one who has signed an agreement with the union promising to meet

to the road as a puppeteer after he was forty. He has toured schools in Oklahoma and Texas for over twenty-five years with a program combining music and puppetry. The children who eagerly await his annual visit with a new show would never suspect that the youthful Parsons has just turned seventy!

The Japanese puppeteer Bungoro continued to perform in Osaka until he was ninety, although he was almost blind. So great was his artistry in moving the female characters in the Bunraku theatre that the Japanese government

Alfred Wallace in his show-biz puppet days (1945).

Martin Stevens in The Toymaker *film.*

union standards and working conditions in all contracts made for clients. Union members are not permitted to work for an agent, ad agency, film producer, television station, or other "employer" who has not signed the union agreement. The names of such firms are posted on an Unfair List until such time as they do sign. The restrictions were set up to protect the performers from unscrupulous business management.

A puppeteer's age is no handicap. One may begin a career or retire at any time. Lewis Parsons, a music teacher from Michigan, took

declared him a "national treasure" while he was still alive.

Not everyone who enters puppetry as a profession will remain for a lifetime. Some puppeteers tire of traveling; others find more satisfying or lucrative careers in other fields. You might discover that an antique dealer, a watercolor instructor, a filmmaker, a foreign-language professor, a toy sculptor, or an environmental activist had been a former puppeteer.

Alfred Wallace was a show-biz puppeteer and Puppetry Consultant for The Association of Junior Leagues. He teamed with Martin

Stevens to make a series of puppet films: Stop and Go, the Safety Twins, were featured marionettes in a series for the J. C. Penney Company: *The Toymaker* series featured Spots and Stripes (hand puppets) with Martin Stevens in the title role. Today Wallace is a full-time filmmaker and distributor (live action and animated films as well as puppets) for his company, Pictura Film Distribution Corp. of New York City.

Martin Stevens started as an actor in tent shows and stock companies before turning to puppets as his "costume and makeup" disguise. He was noted for his playwriting and acting for productions of *The Nativity* and *The Passion Play*. He launched his movie-making career with films for the State Department and for Coronet Films, Chicago. Today "Steve" sends six companies of Stevens Puppets on the road, while he and his wife, Margi, devote their time to painting.

A Midwesterner of my acquaintance stated flatly that he could not imagine himself doing puppets "after forty." He had been trained to tour a public relations puppet show for The Good Teeth Council of Chicago. After that experience he leaped to his own daily television show on a major station in the Southwest. When the series ended, he became an insurance salesman and later a district manager. He left the field before he was forty and claimed that his four children would never see him with a puppet on his hand.

The following examples will introduce the reader to some of the names and faces behind the puppet disguise, and to the varied ways in which they work.

Erica Melchior is a glamorous puppeteer and an astute businesswoman. She credits her skill in puppet-making to her father, who taught her how to handle tools when she was a girl. Erica's first puppets were made to entertain her daughter Peggy and small friends, but soon she was in demand throughout the community. The next step was to learn about agents, develop an act, and take to the road for short stints to polish and perfect her stage presence before an audience. She is now a top attraction at shopping centers, department stores, trade fairs, and nightclubs, as well as being a featured shipboard entertainer on ocean cruises. Cleveland's May Company Department Store built the Snowflake Theatre for her appearance there one season. Erica has performed in France, Germany, Sweden, and Mexico. Always perfecting and adding routines, Erica created marionettes of Diana Ross, Cher, and Barbra Streisand for her Bicentennial Stars. Erica and her Streisand on strings made promotional appearances at shopping centers for the Streisand movie *A Star Is Born*. When daughter Peggy grew up, she learned to do her mother's act with the same glamorous grace, and now there are plans to include granddaughter Heidi when she is old enough to pull the strings.

Rufus and Margo Rose—The late Rufus Rose was a modern-day Geppetto. Pinocchio (whose innocent imp voice was supplied by Margo in their production) was one of his favorite characters. Like Geppetto, "Rufie's" affection for puppets and puppeteers was so great that he became the unofficial Dean of Puppetry in the United States. Rufus and Margo worked first for Tony Sarg, then toured the United States with their own productions of children's classics until 1941. They made the first feature-length film with marionettes, *Jerry Pulls the Strings*, for the American Can Company, and later made others for television release. In 1958 Rufus Rose received the Peabody Award for the best children's television program of the season, *The Blue Fairy*, a daily series based on the adventures of Pinocchio. Rose was the puppet-producer-director for the *Howdy Doody* show on NBC television from 1951 until it closed in 1960. Margo and son Jim are involved in the current revival of *Howdy Doody*, which was created by Buffalo Bob Smith. Rufus served for eight years in the Connecticut General Assembly, and, with Margo, was a founding Trustee of The Eugene O'Neill Memorial Theatre in Waterford. The Roses shared their talents generously with students at The National Theatre Institute and The Theatre of the Deaf, both based at the

PHOTO: ROBERT L. PERRY

Pinocchio from The Blue Fairy *television series by Rufus Rose.*

PHOTO: ROBERT L. PERRY

Rufus Rose, a memorable puppeteer.

COURTESY MARGO ROSE

Margo Rose, sculptress, costumer, and sensitive manipulator.

PHOTO: CLEVELAND NEWS (1946), REPRINT COURTESY THE PLAIN DEALER

Helen Haiman Joseph, the exuberant "puppetess."

PHOTO: JOHN PATRICK HUNT

Bill Baird

COURTESY HAZELLE ROLLINS

Hazelle Rollins, a leading manufacturer of marionettes and hand puppets.

ASSOCIATED PHOTOGRAPHY, SHAKER HEIGHTS, OHIO

Bob Vesely (standing) and Roger Dennis, The Poppinjay Puppets.

COURTESY STEVE HANSEN

Steve Hansen, with Mallard Fillmore.

O'Neill. During the 1976 P of A Festival, Governor Ella Grasso of Connecticut and Puppeteers Burr Tillstrom (through Kukla and Ollie) and Bil Baird paid tribute as one of the O'Neill buildings was dedicated as The Rufus and Margo Rose Theatre.

Helen Haiman Joseph—I am indebted to the Editor of *The Vassar Quarterly* for permission to quote from the charming essay "The World of Puppets" by Helen Joseph (July, 1935).

It is a strange beginning to this story, but a true one. I never saw a marionette in my childhood. Moreover, had I been a better actor of minor parts at the Cleveland Playhouse in its pioneer days when we were all doing something there, it is probable that I should have continued playing maids' and visitors' and, later, old ladies' roles to this day! But after struggling with me through several dramas the director of our little theatre inquired: 'How would you like to work with the marionette group?' We were both relieved at this tactful solution of the problem. And so, all unsuspectingly, I began making and manipulating puppets in a marionette production of *The Death of Tintagiles* presented in Cleveland over twenty years ago; and I happily continued for years working with and later directing the Play House marionette group.

It was after her history *A Book of Marionettes* was published that Mrs. Joseph toured Europe for almost three years visiting the puppet theatres of many countries as a welcome guest. Following the death of her husband, Mrs. Joseph turned to her friends, the puppets, for a profession. Her favorite character, Little Mr. Clown, was the subject of a children's book and also was marketed as a marionette.

I was privileged to see Mrs. Joseph's productions of *Pinocchio* and *Robin Hood* when I was growing up, and later I worked with her during the three summers she was Director of the Puppet Theatre at Cain Park Theatre. As I came to know her as one of the great ladies of puppetry, I understood that the living stage could not contain her magnificent wit, her unerring style, her sophistication, and her mar-velous theatrics. On the puppet stage she was a marvel, and, as a director, she knew how to extract the last ounce of movement and meaning from a script.

The Wicked Queen in *Snow White* was a favorite role of hers. In the final scene, when the Mirror speaks of Snow White's superior beauty, Helen's marionette of the Wicked Queen stormed back and forth across the stage shouting, "I shall die of rage and envy! I shall die of rage and envy!", whereupon she collapsed in a heap and died. After a moment, the Queen's head would rise, turn to the audience and announce, "I am dead." It was Helen's way of getting in the last humorous word.

Bil Baird—The Baird marionettes (and hand puppets) have appeared in all media from Radio City Music Hall to Broadway musicals, to television specials, to Hollywood's *Sound of Music.* His educational films on mathematics, cereals, and telephones find continued use. His permanent theatre on Barrow Street in New York City is open for seasonal runs of productions, which also tour.

Poppinjay Puppets—Roger Dennis and Bob Vesely are popular part-time puppeteers working as The Poppinjay Puppets (Cleveland). They travel and perform only on weekends or holidays (the prime time for sponsored children's fare.) During the week the two partners pursue separate vocations. Each season the Poppinjays produce another fairy tale classic with original script and taped music and voices. They have built their reputation and their repertoire simultaneously, and their tours have expanded from local, to state, to regional bookings. Puppetry will be a full-time career when they retire from their present jobs. A national tour will be no problem, for their careful planning and steady growth have set the stage for it.

In the field of education, the following are notable.

Fern Ellen Zwickey—For thirty-two years Fern Zwickey was a vital force in the Art Education Department of Wayne State University, inspiring art teachers and others with her imaginative approach until she retired in 1969.

The Art Education Building was the meeting place for the Detroit Puppeteers Guild, which she helped found in 1946. She is still the much beloved columnist "Mrs. Z" for the *Guild Newsletter* and an active workshop leader.

Pamela Ritch—A teacher of puppetry and creative drama in the Theatre Department of Illinois State University, Ms. Ritch studied under Aurora Valentinetti at the University of Washington. Her interest in integrating all the arts into the curriculum of childhood education will lead her to a doctoral study in that area at The University of Texas.

Bruce Chessé—Bruce Chessé's background includes a famous father, Ralph Chessé, who was a pioneer in the serious use of the marionette for adult drama. Bruce assisted in his father's productions for stage and television. Bruce Chessé is a free-lance Puppetry Specialist and Consultant to educational systems (California, Puerto Rico, Alaska) and has been a guest lecturer on puppetry at Gothenberg University in Sweden. His book on polyfoam puppets (see Bibliography) offers lively possibilities for classroom learning situations.

Frank Ballard—Professor Ballard heads the Puppetry program in the Theatre Department of the University of Connecticut at Storrs, one of the few institutions to offer an advanced degree in the field. Dr. Ballard has been a major force in expanding theatre awareness of puppetry through his productions with students (*Kismet, The Mikado, The Love of Three Oranges, Peer Gynt, Two by Two*). A two-term President of The Puppeteers of America, Inc., Dr. Ballard is now national Publicity Chairman for the organization. Dr. Ballard invited Albrecht Roser, the famed marionettist from Germany, to be the department's artist-in-residence for a semester in 1977.

Puppeteers in other areas of interest include the following:

Nancy B. Henk is a Crafts and Puppetry Specialist for the City of Detroit Recreation Department. She supervises both summer and winter touring programs, performing herself and hiring part-time assistants whom she trains. The Puppet Wagon, which tours parks during the summer, has two side-opening stages, one for hand puppets and one for marionettes. Plays are supplemented with an impromptu performance by the audience, using stick puppets that the company provides. Winter programs are carried to recreation centers and public library locations and include workshops, demonstrations, and audience participation, as well as performances. For twenty days each December Nancy Henk's troupe provides six shows a day for the city-sponsored Christmas Carnival at Cobo Hall.

Virginia Rivers is head of the Creative Programming Department, Tampa–Hillsborough County Public Library System, organized in 1969. With her staff of three, she creates and presents programs with the emphasis on literature. During 1974 the count was 333 programs reaching 33,523 persons. A new production premieres each month for Family Night in the Library's 200-seat dome-shaped auditorium. Special performances are arranged for schoolchildren, who are brought to the library during school hours two days a week. Other programming includes Mini Puppet shows: one puppet and a storyteller, no stage; story hours; creative dramatics; Impromptu Theatre; and Guest Artists from the Community. Mrs. Rivers' group tours the fourteen city-county branches bimonthly. The department also circulates Program Kits for use by other public libraries throughout the state (for postage charges). The kits include full-scale puppet productions that provide everything needed for the show except the stage.

PERMANENT PUPPET THEATRES

The permanent puppet theatre in the United States has been the most difficult proposition for puppeteers to sustain. The stability of a fixed location has obvious advantages, and the challenge of educating an audience to the vast possibilities of the puppet stage is also attractive. The public needs more than the chance encounter with a puppet show or the weekly puppet format on television to fully understand the depth and breadth of the art. There

Fern Zwickey.

Pamela Ritch.

Bruce Chessé.

Dr. Frank Ballard.

Rod puppets for the musical production To a Tea, *copyrighted 1976 by Zuby & Babisch, built by students in the art classes of Joe Babisch and Elaine Juhasz, Youngstown State University.*

Nancy B. Henk.

Virginia Rivers.

is a need for an adult puppet theatre, separate from the one that serves children, to stretch the audience mind in the way that films, dance, and theatre attempt to do. Those puppeteers who are trying to give the puppet a home where it can take root and grow strong have a dream of an age when puppetry can flower in a way we have not seen.

The Yale Puppeteers, Walton & O'Rourke, and C. Ray Smith each had a turn at a theatre located in Los Angeles' Olvera Street. The Yale Puppeteers established The Turnabout Theatre on La Cienega Boulevard in Los

end to the famed puppet opera at the Kungsholm Theatre Restaurant in Chicago. Louisa Mustin built a puppet theatre in Augusta, Georgia, but was not able to continue it beyond a few seasons, and even Cheryl Crawford's presentation of Burr Tillstrom's Kuklapolitans at the old Astor Hotel lasted a shorter time than expected. Puppeteers have courage, and they continue to try.

The Perch Puppeteers (Ames, Iowa)

Veronika Ruedenberg and Nancy Kegley maintained a theatre on Main Street for several

COURTESY THE PERCH PUPPETEERS

Nancy Kegley and Veronika Ruedenberg.

COURTESY THE PERCH PUPPETEERS

Human and puppets cast their shadows for "Max and Mortiz," based on a German comic strip.

Angeles and ran continuously for thirteen years. Stages at both ends of the theatre, and trolley car seats in between (which were flipped over to face the other stage during intermission), allowed the audience to see the opening show with Harry Burnett's marionettes, followed by a revue with live performers and Forman Brown at the piano. Elsa Lanchester, Dorothy Neumann, and Lotte Goslar were among the "guest artists" in the live revue. An attempt to transplant the Turnabout to San Francisco came to a disappointing close. A change of management brought an

seasons and developed an audience of sophisticated patrons for their imaginative work, which ranged from Alfred Jarry's *Ubu Roi* (a magnificent multimedia presentation) to Grimm's fairy tale "Mother Holly," to The Second Shepherd's Play, to originals, including *The Planet of the Grapes,* which double-cast the characters so that they could appear either as marionettes or on a shadow screen for special interplanetary effects. They also combined live shadows with shadow puppets and a live jug band for "Max and Moritz" based on the German comic strip by W. Busch. The local audience came to anticipate the excitement of each new production, which might use hand, rod, stick, shadow, and string puppets with music, dance, pantomime, live acting, and audience participation. The Perch Puppeteers are now primarily a touring group, not because they lacked success, but because of building code restrictions.

Pemrad Puppets (Lansing, Michigan)

Phyllis E. Maner and Rhea A. Dow (their

and have used their organizational training to bring the puppet arts to their community.

Lovelace Theatre (Pittsburgh, Pennsylvania)

After a twelve-year run at its small theatre and museum on Ellsworth Avenue, the Lovelace Theatre moved to a new home at the Museum of Art Theatre at Carnegie Institute, with a season premiere (February 19, 1977) of David Visser's *Ragtime and All That Jazz,* combining puppets, actors, slide projections,

PHOTO: TOM TURK, WKAR-TV

Phyllis E. Maner and Rhea A. Dow, Pemrad Puppets.

initials form the company name) incorporated as a nonprofit group in order to receive grants to sponsor the 1973 P of A Festival on the Michigan State University campus at East Lansing. During the school year, they import professional productions for performances at a local high school. In 1976 they received a grant for a Bicentennial multimedia project with puppets, dance, the Lansing Symphony, and volunteer puppeteers from their organization. Both Mrs. Maner and Mrs. Dow worked with their local Junior League Puppet Group

lighting effects, and a montage of jazz styles. Margo Lovelace, who founded the company in 1953, has studied puppet theatres in Russia and Japan and has produced plays by Michel de Ghelderode, Cocteau, and Giraudoux as well as classic tales for children.

Puppet Playhouse (New Orleans, Louisiana)

Nancy Staub, director of the Playhouse, founded the group in 1968 using a small theatre seating 60. It has since moved to the 225-seat theatre at the New Orleans Museum of

Art, playing 50 performances a year, with 100 more on tour. She also collaborates with the New Orleans Philharmonic Symphony to present an annual Kinderkonzert. A total audience of over 40,000 comes to see the three or four productions each year. The company is dedicated to utilizing subject matter that can deeply involve the audience, rather than merely entertain. A local reviewer, after seeing the performance of *Ananse the Spider,* wrote: "I propose Nancy be dubbed a civic treasure."

opened August 13, 1976, with Bruce D. Schwartz as guest artist. Performances by guest and resident companies will fill the season. The theatre includes a gallery for the display of a permanent collection and temporary exhibitions.

Puppet Show Place (Brookline Village, Massachusetts)

Mary Churchill and a staff of three are the resident company (The Cranberry Puppeteers)

PHOTO: JOHN KUBACKI

Christopher, George, and Michael Latshaw (left to right) peer out from behind some of the disguises they have used on the puppet stage.

Nancy Staub is the current President of The Puppeteers of America, Inc., and served as Festival Chairman when the group met at Tulane University in August 1974.

National Puppet Center (Olde Town Alexandria, Virginia)

Allan Stevens, for seven years Director of the Smithsonian Resident and National Touring Companies, and Judy A. K. Holets, Executive Producer, restored an old 300-seat vaudeville/movie house for their venture, which

in a small theatre seating 150. Six matinees are offered each weekend of the year and during holiday weeks, with a standard admission of $1.00 for all ages to encourage parents to attend with their children. Selected guest companies alternate with the Cranberry Puppeteers to vary the bill. The quality of programming has built a brisk business and a loyal following.

On the West Coast one might find Bob Baker Marionettes performing in the round at his party center. Bob Baker and partner Alton

Wood also create many puppetlike special effects for Hollywood films. The Park and Recreation Board sponsors Children's Fairland in Oakland, California, where Lewis Mahlmann is the resident puppeteer. For a time, the Universal Studio tours featured a stop to see Tony Urbano and his marionettes perform.

The people who choose puppetry as a career have three things in common: training, talent, and tenacity. It is this combination that keeps the art alive as the ultimate disguise.

Arnott, Peter D. *Plays Without People*. Bloomington: Indiana University Press, 1964.

Baird, Bil. *The Art of the Puppet*. New York: Macmillan, 1965.

Batchelder, Marjorie. *The Puppet Theatre Handbook*. New York: Harper & Row, Publishers, 1947.

Batchelder, Marjorie, and Comer, Virginia Lee. *Puppets and Plays: A Creative Approach*. New York: Harper & Brothers, Publishers, 1965.

Beaumont, Cyril W. *Puppets and Puppetry*. London, New York: Studio Publications, 1958.

Böhmer, Günter. *The Wonderful World of Puppets,* trans. by Gerald Morice, based on the Puppet Collection of the City of Munich. Boston: Plays, Inc., 1971.

Boylan, Eleanor. *Puppet Plays for Special Days*. Rowayton, CT: New Plays for Children, 1974.

Bramall, Eric. *Puppet Plays and Playwriting*. London: G. Bell & Sons Ltd, 1961.

Brhalji-Merin, Oto. *Great Masks,* trans. by Herma Plummer. New York: N. H. Abrams, 1971.

Brown, Forman. *The Pie-eyed Piper, and other impertinent plays for puppets*. New York: Greenburg, 1933.

————. *Punch's Progress*. New York: Macmillan, 1936.

Chessé, Bruce, and Armstrong, Beverly. *Puppets from Polyfoam: SPONGEES*. 1975. Early Stages Publications, P. O. Box 5027, Walnut Creek, CA 94596.

Cummings, Richard. *101 Hand Puppets*. New York: David McKay Company, Inc., 1962.

Drama Review, The. Issues T38 Winter 1968 and T47 (no date), articles on the Bread and Puppet Theatre.

Engler, Larry, and Fijan, Carol. *Making Puppets Come Alive*. New York: Taplinger Publishing Company, 1973.

Fettig, Hansjürgen. *Hand and Rod Puppets*. English version by John Wright and Susanne Forster. Boston: Plays, Inc., 1973.

Fling, Helen. Marionettes, *How to Make and Work Them*. New York: Dover Publications, Inc., 1973.

Fraser, Peter. *Introducing Puppetry*. New York: Watson-Guptill Publications, 1968.

French, Susan. *Presenting Marionettes*. New York: Reinhold Publishing Corp., 1964.

Grater, Michael. *Paper People*. New York: Taplinger Publishing, 1969.

Halas, John, and Manvell, Roger. *Design in Motion*. New York: Hastings House Publishers, 1962.

Joseph, Helen Haiman. *A Book of Marionettes*. New York: B. W. Huebsch, 1920.

Keene, Donald. *Bunraku: the art of the Japanese puppet theatre*. Tokyo: Kodansha International Ltd. (Distributed by Japan Publications Trading Co., Rutland, Vermont), 1965.

Kline, Peter. *The Theatre Student: The Actor's Voice*. New York: Richards Rosen Press, Inc., 1972.

Lano, David. *A Wandering Showman, I*. East Lansing: Michigan State University Press, 1957.

Lipman, Jean, ed., with Nancy Foote. *Calder's Circus*. New York: E. P. Dutton & Co., Inc., in association with the Whitney Museum of American Art, 1972.

Mahlmann, Lewis, and Jones, David Cadwalader. *Puppet Plays for Young Players.* Boston: Plays, Inc., 1974.

McPharlin, Paul. *The Puppet Theatre in America: A History: 1524 to Now.* With a supplement, *Puppets in America Since 1948,* by Marjorie Batchelder McPharlin. Boston: Plays, Inc., 1969.

Meilach, Dona Z. *Soft Sculptures and Other Soft Art Forms.* New York: Crown Publishers, Inc., 1974.

Nicoll, Allardyce. *Masks, Mimes and Miracles.* New York: Cooper Square Publishers, 1963.

Obraztsov, Sergei. *The Chinese Puppet Theatre.* London: Faber and Faber, 1961.

————. *My Profession,* trans. by Ralph Parker and Valentina Scott. Moscow: Foreign Languages Publishing House, 1950.

Open Stage Technical Manual. 1964. Prepared by James Hull Miller, 3415 Reily Lane, Shreveport, LA 71105. (Miller's ideas on free-standing construction are adaptable as puppet environments.)

Paludan, Lis. *Playing with Puppets.* Trans. by Christone Crowley. Boston: Plays, Inc., 1974.

Pinocchio. Adapted by George Latshaw. Chicago: The Coach House Press, 1959.

Pinocchio for the Stage. Dramatized and illustrated by Remo Bufano. New York: Alfred A. Knopf, 1929.

Puppet Theatre of the Modern World, The. Compiled by the Editorial Board of UNIMA under the chairmanship of Margareta Niculescu, 1st American ed. Boston: Plays, Inc., 1967.

Rawson, Ruth. *The Theatre Student: Acting.* New York: Richards Rosen Press, Inc., 1970.

Reiniger, Lotte. *Shadow Theatres and Shadow Films.* New York: Watson-Guptill Publications, 1970.

Riley, Olive, *Masks and Magic.* New York: Studio Publications and Thomas Y. Crowell Company, 1955.

Rottger, Ernst. *Creative Paper Design.* New York: Reinhold Publishing Corp., 1961.

Schönewolf, Herta. *Play with Light and Shadow.* New York: Reinhold Book Corporation, 1968.

Severn, Bill. *Shadow Magic.* New York: David McKay Company, 1959.

Simmen, Rene. *The World of Puppets.* New York: Thomas Y. Crowell Company, 1975.

Spolin, Viola. *Improvisation for the Theater.* Evanston: Northwestern University Press, 1963.

Theatre Crafts. "Puppetry for the Theatre." Special issue: March/April 1975.

Periodicals

Cartoonist Profiles
Craft Horizons
Communication Arts
Dance Magazine
Graphis
Print
Theatre Crafts

Organizations
The Puppeteers of America, Inc.
Mrs. Olga Stevens, Executive Secretary
P. O. Box 1061
Ojai, CA 93023

The Puppetry Journal
Don Avery, Editor
2015 Novem Drive
Fenton, MO 63026

UNIMA–USA (*Union Internationale de la Marionette*)
Mollie P. Falkenstein, General Secretary, First Vice-President of UNIMA
132 Chiquita Street
Laguna Beach, CA 92651